Nice Talking with You 2

Student's Book

Tom Kenny

CAMBRIDGE
UNIVERSITY PRESS

Acknowledgments

The author would like to thank Jane Fancher for sharing her talent as a writer and performer. The energy and creativity she brings to a project always makes work seem less like work and more like fun, which is how it ought to be. Thanks also to the students of Nagoya University of Foreign Studies, who over the years this book was in development patiently allowed me to test it on them and let me see what helped them and what just didn't work. To Robert Habbick, Nancy Mutoh, Kazuhiko Matsuno, David K. Jeffrey, Shigeji Ishiguro, Dan Parker, Elaine Kenny, Chuck Rand, and *consigliere* Frank Parker: know that nothing gets done without your support, encouragement, and inspiration.

The author thanks all the team at Cambridge University Press, in particular: Richard Walker, editor par excellence and the most professional, insightful, and diligent individual an author could hope to work with; Katherine Wong, for her design expertise and constant attention to detail during the production phase; and Keiko Sugiyama, for her work on the illustrations.

Shout-outs to colleagues and fellow teachers for their contributions and support for the *Nice Talking With You* project, most notably Philip Rush, Brian McNeill, Trevor Astley, Masahiro Kato, Rebecca Brinkley, Louise Haynes, Brad Deacon, Suzanne Miyake, Simon Lees, Tanja Kondo, Philip Suthons, Yoshi Sato, Troy Miller, Matt Lott, Claudia Bracco, Joshua Wilson, and Chihiro Yonekawa.

Finally, love to my most treasured conversation partners, Rotalyn and Kira.

Book and cover design by Albert Tan.

Illustrations by Li Dan Illustration & Design Studio, Richard Peter David, and Albert Tan.

The author and publishers would like to thank Richard LePage and Associates for their work on the audio recording and production, and the following for permission to reproduce photographs:

p. 12, (*Clockwise from top left*) ©iStockphoto.com/toxawww, ©iStockphoto.com/pink_cotton_candy, ©iStockphoto.com/Vadymvdrobot, ©iStockphoto.com/spfoto, p. 28, (*Clockwise from top left*) ©iStockphoto.com/muratseyit, ©iStockphoto.com/peepo, ©iStockphoto.com/travelif, ©iStockphoto.com/AndrewJohnson, ©iStockphoto.com/dogayusufdokdok, ©iStockphoto.com/dave9296, ©iStockphoto.com/kreci, ©iStockphoto.com/mediaphotos, p. 44, (*Clockwise from top left*) ©iStockphoto.com/double_p, ©iStockphoto.com/si_arts, ©iStockphoto.com/jhorrocks, ©iStockphoto.com/izusek, ©iStockphoto.com/Cybermama, p. 57 (*Clockwise from top left*) ©iStockphoto.com/LindaJohnsonbaugh, ©iStockphoto.com/leezsnow, ©iStockphoto.com/profeta, ©iStockphoto.com/foment, ©iStockphoto.com/AVAVA, p. 109, (*Clockwise from top left*) ©iStockphoto.com/craftvision, ©iStockphoto.com/CreativeFire, ©iStockphoto.com/leezsnow, ©iStockphoto.com/adventtr, ©iStockphoto.com/jcarillet

Contents

Welcome to
Nice Talking with You

What's different about *Nice Talking with You*?

Nice Talking with You is different from other books that you may have used before. There are no dialogues to memorize. Instead, this book will help you to have **real conversations**: conversations about you and your friends that help you make and keep relationships with other people. This kind of conversation is very common in all languages, because making and keeping relationships with others is the most important function of spoken language.

How will *Nice Talking with You* help improve my English?

- You'll review **vocabulary** you have probably learned before, but have probably never used in conversation.

- You'll **practice speaking** with easy topics, using basic questions, in **timed conversations**.

- You'll learn how to **get ready** for conversations and get practice **noticing** the English you and your partners use.

- You'll hear a **wide variety of English** – native speakers from around the world, even non-native speakers of English.

- Most of all, you'll master some important phrases and expresssions that will make your conversations smoother and more natural. We call these **conversation strategies**.

What is the goal of the unit?

You will speak English using the new conversation strategies you've learned.

What is the goal of the course?

By the end of this book, you'll be able to use all the conversation strategies you've learned naturally and automatically.

Good luck and have fun!

Tom Kenny

How a unit works

Each unit contains a carefully controlled sequence of activities, which build upon each other. The different sections and their functions are shown below.

Likes and dislikes

This is a short, personalized, warm-up activity to focus students' attention on the topic. Typically, students read the statements and check the boxes.

Words and phrases

Approximately 30 key words and phrases related to the unit topic are introduced here. Students first get a chance to check if they understand them and then are given focused practice by doing the activities **Match it**, **Fill it in**, and **Put it together** on the following page.

Conversation questions

Commonly used questions related to the topic are introduced and practiced in this section. **Watch out!** raises students' awareness of common mistakes; the **Language point** provides a short, one-point Focus on Form; and **PRACTICE** gives students the opportunity to check their understanding of the **Language point**.

Conversation strategies

Key conversation strategies that help students manage conversations more effectively are introduced and practiced on these two pages. For each strategy introduced, several high-frequency expressions are highlighted in model conversations. Students are then given a chance to practice these in a controlled manner.

Conversation listening

Students listen to three or four short conversations on the unit topic, which feature the conversation strategies and vocabulary previously introduced. There are three listening stages:

A First listening This provides listening for gist
B Second listening This focuses students' attention on key details
C Noticing the conversation strategies This last stage is designed to raise students' awareness of the strategies used by the speakers.

Get ready!

This section serves to consolidate the vocabulary, question patterns, and conversation strategies highlighted in the unit. Students are given a chance to plan for their conversation by writing notes and relevant language in the boxes provided.

Do it!

Students are now ready to put it all together and practice one or more timed conversations with their partners. They are also encouraged to write down expressions and/or word and phrases they notice their partner using.

Real conversations

Real conversations gives students addition listening practice on the topic. These feature unscripted conversations between native and non-native English speakers from around the world, giving students exposure to a variety of English accents.

Thinking about . . .

This last section of the unit encourages students to think critically about aspects of the unit topic. Activities are carefully scaffolded to ensure that even low level students are able to succeed.

More resources

Web site www.nicetalkingwithyou.com

Free additional resources for students and teachers can be found on the Web site. The complete audio program in MP3 file format is available to download and listen to. Students are also able to listen to Global Voices. These are authentic, unscripted monologues related to the unit topics, spoken by native and non-native speakers of English.

Teacher's Manual

The Teacher's Manual offers comprehensive, step-by-step teaching notes for all sections of the book, as well as providing a wealth of practical teaching tips. It also contains the answers to all exercises and audio scripts of the Conversation listening sections.

Long time no see

Likes and dislikes

When you meet an old friend, what do you like to talk about? Look at the topics below and put checks (✔) in the boxes.

Topic	Like	Not sure	Don't like
Where you live			
Your family/romantic life			
Your job			
How much money you make			
Your friend's appearance			
Friends you both know			

www.nicetalkingwithyou.com
Share your likes and dislikes with other people like you.

Words and phrases

Check the meaning of these words and phrases. Then use them to do the activities on the next page.

age	death	haircut	lost	special
anyone	fiancé(e)	house	new baby	spoken
at home	full-time job	illness	promotion	surgery
birth	grad school	kids	propose	traveling
college	graduate	live	remember	weight
dating	grown-up	look great	see	worn-out

Match it

Match the word on the left with the meaning on the right. Write the letter on the line. Then check your answers with a partner.

1. _____ fiancé(e)   a) the end of life
2. _____ kids   b) when the body or mind is not well
3. _____ grown-up   c) someone who is engaged to be married
4. _____ death   d) not normal or usual
5. _____ special   e) children
6. _____ ill   f) not childish

Fill it in

Use the words and phrases on page 7 to complete the sentences. Then check your answers with a partner.

1. I have been _____ in the same apartment for five years.

2. Do you _____ that guy I was with? He _____ to me on New Year's Eve!

3. Sarah was hoping for a _____, but her company had a bad year.

4. I was hired as a part-time worker, but once I _____ they have promised to give me a _____ _____.

5. John has really been _____ a lot for his work.

6. You are _____ _____! That new _____ really suits you.

7. My brother has a _____ _____, and his wife is trying hard to exercise.

8. Max is working _____ _____ this month because he had knee _____.

Put it together

Draw a line to put the sentences together.

1. Tell me,   why don't you come over to my house?

2. I don't really like change. I've lived   with Britney at all since graduation.

3. I want to teach at a college level, so   in the same city since birth.

4. When you have some time,   are you seeing anyone special?

5. I haven't spoken   I am applying to grad school.

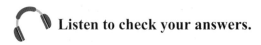 **Listen to check your answers.**

Conversation questions

> How have you been?
> What have you been doing?
> How long has it been?

Practice asking and answering the questions above with different partners.

Watch out!

Be careful not to make these common mistakes.

✗	✔
~~I have been doing working.~~	I have been working.
~~I got baby girl/boy.~~	I have a baby now, a little girl/boy.
~~You look same.~~	You look the same. / You haven't changed a bit.

Practice saying these out loud so you can remember them!

Language point

Forms of be: am/is/are   was/were   has/have been

I **am** working part-time.

We **were** in the same class at high school.

He **has been** working at a big company since last year.

PRACTICE

Write the correct form of the verb *be* on the lines below.

1. We _____ going to have a baby next month.

2. My daughter _____ in 4th grade.

3. Her boyfriend _____ in a band for two years.

4. They _____ traveling in Southeast Asia since March.

5. My parents _____ very pleased when I graduated.

Conversation strategies

Getting someone's attention

Use the expression below to begin talking with someone. It's a polite way to get their attention.

Excuse me . . .

Excuse me, aren't you Jane?

Yes, I am. Do we know each other?

PRACTICE

With a partner, use *Excuse me* to get someone's attention. Then practice these questions and responses.

Question	Response
1. Don't I know you?	Um, I'm not sure
2. Aren't you . . . ?	Yes, I am.
3. Haven't we met before?	Yes, I think so.

TIP Use *Pardon me?* if you want your partner to repeat something.

Starting a "catch-up" conversation

Use the expressions below to begin a conversation to catch up on an old friend's life.

Wow, long time no see!

It's been a while.
It's been a long time.
It's been ages.

How are things?
How have you been?

Jane! Oh my gosh, long time no see! How have you been?

Great. I've been traveling around the world.

PRACTICE

Look at the list of topics below. Match them to the sentences on the right.

Appearance   I'm living in Tokyo.
Job   I'm married now, and we have two kids.
Relationships   These days, I'm working for Google.
Where   You haven't changed a bit! You look great!

Now practice short catch-up conversations using the sentences and expressions above.

Pre-closing a conversation

Use these phrases to show that you're ready to end a conversation.

PRACTICE

Fill in the blanks with your own sentences. Then practice saying them with a partner.

I've really got to . . .

1. get home. *Time to cook dinner!*

2. go to work. _____

3. meet someone. _____

4. catch a train. _____

 TIP Remember to say *How about you?* if you want to ask your partner the question they asked you.

Closing a conversation

These are some useful phrases to close your conversation.

PRACTICE

Work with a partner. Use all the strategies on pages 10 and 11 to practice a complete conversation.

Conversation listening

A First listening

Listen to the conversations. Is the main speaker married, single, or divorced? How many children do they have? Put checks (✔) in the boxes and write on the lines.

1.
- ☐ married
- ☐ single
- ☐ divorced
- _____ no. of children

3.
- ☐ married
- ☐ single
- ☐ divorced
- _____ no. of children

2.
- ☐ married
- ☐ single
- ☐ divorced
- _____ no. of children

4.
- ☐ married
- ☐ single
- ☐ divorced
- _____ no. of children

B Second listening

What other information do the speakers give about themselves? Read the statements below. Write T if they are true and F if they are false.

1. a) They used to work together.   _____
    b) She hasn't changed her appearance.   _____

2. a) He loves his job at Auto Zone.   _____
    b) He has been working weekends for 10 years.   _____

3. a) They lived in the same neighborhood when they were children.   _____
    b) He exercises for 30 minutes a day.   _____

4. a) They knew each other in high school.   _____
    b) She is working for a training company.   _____

C Noticing the conversation strategies

Listen for the pre-closing phrases. What reasons do the speakers give for ending the conversation? Number the reasons in the order you hear them. One is not used.

_____ meeting someone

_____ not being late for work

_____ going home for dinner

_____ going to the gym

_____ catching a train

Get ready!

Organize your questions, answers, and vocabulary here to get ready for your *Long time no see* conversation.

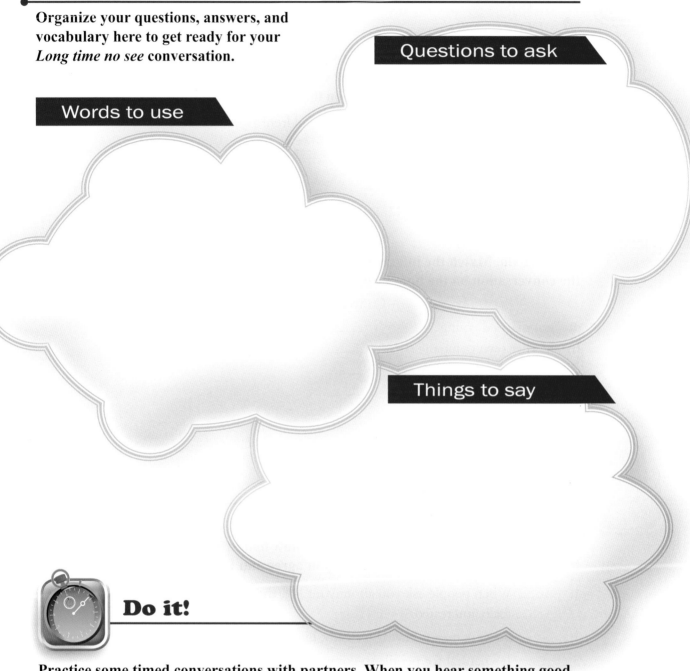

Questions to ask

Words to use

Things to say

Do it!

Practice some timed conversations with partners. When you hear something good, write it on this page after your conversation so you can remember it!

Noticing my partner's English

Real conversations

A Listening

Listen to three short conversations between old friends meeting again after several years. Are the speakers married or not? Circle Y for Yes or N for No. How many children do they say they have? Write on the lines.

	Married?	Children?
Conversation 1	Y / N	_____
Conversation 2	Y / N	_____
Conversation 3	Y / N	_____

B Vocabulary

Listen again. Match the information with each conversation. Write the number of the conversation on the lines below.

Conversation

a) got married young   _____
b) has her own company   _____
c) live nearby each other   _____
d) looks the same as before   _____
e) loves children   _____
f) is a student   _____

Thinking about . . .

What people really think

How interested are we in others' lives, and how honest are we about our own? Read the statements below. Write A if you agree and D if you disagree.

1. _____ When people ask you about your life, they're just being polite. They're not really interested.

2. _____ Success means having a steady, high-paying job, a family, and a nice home.

3. _____ It's natural for people to compare their status or appearance with others.

4. _____ People often exaggerate or lie about their lives in "Long time no see" situations.

5. _____ It's impolite to ask someone why they're not married or why they don't have children.

PRACTICE

Share your opinions with your partner.

> I think a high-status job is one of the best things to have.

> Really? I think having a family matters most.

www.nicetalkingwithyou.com

Share your opinions with people your age. Listen to Global Voices to hear what English speakers around the world have to say.

My place

Likes and dislikes

What's the area or place you live in like? Write T for True and F for False on the lines below. How much do you like it? Put a check (✔) in one of the boxes.

I live in an area that has a lot of people. _____

I live in an area that has blue skies, fresh air, and lots of trees. _____

My neighborhood has a lot of old buildings in it. _____

My home isn't too big and isn't too small. _____

My home is bright and sunny. _____

My room is small but clean. _____

	☺	☺	☹	☹	☹
My place:					

www.nicetalkingwithyou.com
Share your likes and dislikes with other people like you.

Words and phrases

Check the meaning of these words and phrases. Then use them to do the activities on the next page.

a walk-up	cozy	hip	spacious
apartment	cramped	messy	studio
basement	doorman	multicultural	swimming pool
bright	elevator	old fashioned	tidy
campus	fireplace	realtor	yard
convenient	garage	roommate	yuppie
shopping	ground floor	secure	
country	gym	senior community	

15

Match it

Match the word on the left with the meaning on the right. Write the letter on the line. Then check your answers with a partner.

1. _____ a walk-up
2. _____ senior community
3. _____ realtor
4. _____ yard
5. _____ roommate
6. _____ basement

a) a person who helps people to buy or sell property
b) an underground floor of a building
c) a neighborhood that only allows residents over 50 years old
d) somebody who shares a room, apartment, or house
e) a building with stairs but not elevators
f) the land surrounding a house; garden

Fill it in

Use the words and phrases on page 15 to complete the sentences. Then check your answers with a partner.

1. Even though I live in a big city, I feel safe in my _____ because of my building's _____.

2. I don't need to go to the _____ anymore, because my new apartment is on the fourth floor and the building doesn't have an _____.

3. I used to live in a _____ _____ apartment, but it wasn't private enough.

4. I live close to the international _____, so the neighborhood is really _____.

5. My _____ is really tiny. I have to be very organized so it doesn't feel _____.

6. I looked at some really nice places with _____ _____, but they were all too expensive.

7. I don't like very modern apartments much. My perfect place would be more _____ _____.

8. My place is really _____ in the morning because my windows face east.

Put it together

Draw a line to put the sentences together.

1. I think country life is peaceful, but
2. I don't want a big house;
3. I used to live with a girl who was
4. Having a dog makes me feel
5. I live close to a lot of tech companies, so

I'd rather have just a few cozy rooms.

a lot of my neighbors are yuppies.

more secure than having an electronic security system.

really messy and never did her dishes.

it would be hard to live without convenient shopping.

 Listen to check your answers.

Conversation questions

> Do you live alone or with your family?
> What's your place like?
> Which do you prefer, staying at home or going out? Why?

Practice asking and answering the questions above with different partners.

Watch out!

Be careful not to make these common mistakes.

✗	✓
~~Do you keep animal?~~	Do you have any pets?
~~I like staying my home.~~	I like staying at home.
~~My place is like small, one room.~~	My place is small; there's just one room.

Practice saying these out loud so you can remember them.

Language point

Prepositions: at   in   on   with

I can shop **at** many stores in my neighborhood.

Our home is **in** the suburbs.

My apartment is **on** the third floor.

I share a place **with** my sister.

PRACTICE

Write the correct preposition on the lines below.

1. We live _____ the top floor of our building.

2. My new apartment is really small, but it's _____ a great neighborhood.

3. I used to live in the country _____ my parents and grandparents.

4. Jon's new roommate spends all his time _____ work.

5. There is an old fireplace _____ the living room.

Conversation strategies

Introducing a new idea

Use this expression to introduce a new idea or invitation.

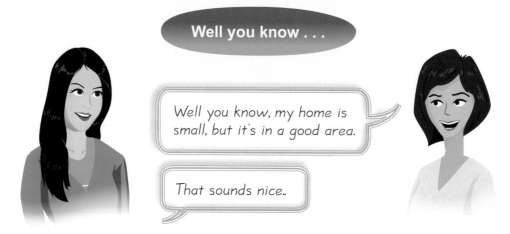

Well you know . . .

Well you know, my home is small, but it's in a good area.

That sounds nice.

Making a general invitation

Use these expressions to make a general invitation.

You should come over **sometime.**
when you're free.
when you're not too busy.

That sounds nice.

Yeah. You should come over sometime. There's a nice park near my house.

PRACTICE

Work with a partner. Use the phrases above to make a general invitation, and then add extra information. Use the examples below. Add your own ideas.

There's a nice park near my house.

We'll cook something.

I'll show you around.

We can play games.

You can play with my dog.

Your ideas: _____

_____

 TIP Repeating something shows your partner that you are listening and interested. For example:

A: You can play with my dog
B: Your dog! What's her name?
A: Summer. She's yellow!

Accepting a general invitation

Use these phrases to accept an invitation. They help you sound positive and friendly.

I'd love to/that.

Good idea!

That would be great.

Sounds great.

Well you know, you should come over when you're not too busy.

Thanks. I'd love to!

PRACTICE

Work with a new partner. Follow the steps below to practice making general invitations as before. This time, use the phrases above to accept the invitation and complete the conversation.

1. Introduce an invitation
2. Make an invitation and add extra information
3. Accept the invitation

Extra information

There's a nice park near my house.

We'll cook something.

I'll show you around.

We can play games.

You can play with my dog.

Your ideas: _____

_____

_____

_____

Conversation listening

A First listening

Listen to the conversations. Number the pictures in the order you hear about them. One is not used.

B Second listening

How do the speakers describe the places they live in? Circle A or B.

1. **A** She lives near the train station.   **B** She lives near the bus station.
2. **A** It has a big backyard.   **B** It has a big kitchen.
3. **A** It's not so small.   **B** It's on the first floor.
4. **A** It's in a quiet area.   **B** It has a swimming pool.

C Noticing the conversation strategies

Listen to the speakers' invitations. What do they invite the people to do? Circle A or B.

1. **A** Take a bus tour in their neighborhood   **B** Visit stores in their neighborhood
2. **A** Check out the backyard   **B** Enjoy some home cooking
3. **A** Play with her cat   **B** Visit her company
4. **A** Have a barbecue   **B** Go swimming

Get ready!

Organize your questions, answers, and vocabulary here to get ready for your *My place* conversation.

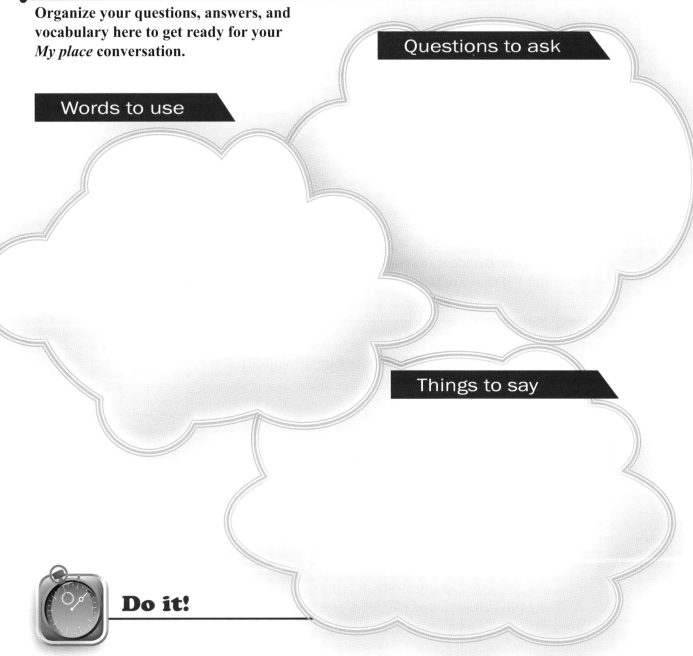

Questions to ask

Words to use

Things to say

Do it!

Practice some timed conversations with partners. When you hear something good, write it on this page after your conversation so you can remember it!

Noticing my partner's English

Real conversations

A Listening

Listen to four short conversations about where people live. Do the speakers live alone or with their families? Check (✔) the boxes below.

		lives alone	lives with family
1.	woman	☐	☐
2.	woman	☐	☐
3.	man	☐	☐
4.	woman	☐	☐

B Vocabulary

Listen again. Decide if the statements below are true or false. Write T if they are true and F if they are false.

1. There's a great view of the night sky from the woman's house. _____

2. All the woman's pets live in the yard outside the house. _____

3. The man has learned skills to take care of himself. _____

4   The woman shares a room with her sister. _____

Thinking about . . .

A nice home

What makes a good place to live? Read the statements below. Write A if you agree and D if you disagree.

A good home . . .

1. _____ is near family members.
2. _____ is convenient for work or school.
3. _____ has clean air and plenty of green trees.
4. _____ is in a high-status neighborhood.
5. _____ is big and expensive.
6. _____ is in a safe area.

PRACTICE

Share your opinions with your partner.

> I think a good home is one that's convenient to get to and near family members and relatives.

> Really? I think safety and status of the neighborhood are more important.

www.nicetalkingwithyou.com

Share your opinions with people your age. Listen to Global Voices to hear what English speakers around the world have to say.

Money

Likes and dislikes

What do you usually spend your money on? Write 1–5 below next to the categories.
(1 = you spend most money on this; 5 = you spend least on this.)

Food and drinks _____   Entertainment _____

Transportation _____   Savings _____

Shopping _____   Bills (phone, Internet, etc.) _____

 www.nicetalkingwithyou.com
Share your likes and dislikes with other people like you.

Words and phrases

Check the meaning of these words and phrases. Then use them to do the activities on the next page.

bank account	discount store	make payments	stock market
budget	financing	online billing	tax
careful	gambling	retail therapy	tipping
cash	generous	savings account	utility bill
check	investment	shopaholic	wholesale
credit card	limited resources	shopping spree	
debit card	live it up	stingy	

Match it

Match the word on the left with the meaning on the right. Write the letter on the line. Then check your answers with a partner.

1. _____ retail therapy
2. _____ shopaholic
3. _____ debit card
4. _____ wholesale
5. _____ savings account
6. _____ tax

a) buying or selling in large quantities at low prices
b) a bank account that earns interest
c) going shopping to improve your mood
d) money paid to the government
e) a person who shops far too much
f) a card that pays directly from a bank account

Fill it in

Use the words and phrases on page 23 to complete the sentences. Then check your answers with a partner.

1. I bought a new car, but I can _____ _____ each month rather than pay it off at once.

2. I set up my _____ _____ to automatically pay all of my regular bills each month, so I don't have to worry about them.

3. Sometimes after a _____ _____ I find I've bought things that I already had.

4. She has _____ _____, so she has to stay on a _____.

5. Christy doesn't trust _____ _____. She uses cash to pay for everything.

6. Tim isn't poor, but he prefers to shop at _____ _____ because he is _____.

7. Ben is really _____ with his money; he is famous for tipping waitresses really well.

8. Lots of people put their savings into the stock market, but you have to remember that you are _____ with your money.

Put it together

Draw a line to put the sentences together.

1. Paying with a check is
2. I like stores that do gift wrapping, because
3. I give part of my salary to a hospital charity.
4. I love online billing, because
5. When you are buying electronics,

it's convenient and saves paper.

it's a good idea to shop around for the best price.

I'm not good at that.

really slow and not very reliable.

I think it's an investment for my health.

Listen to check your answers.

Conversation questions

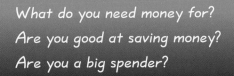

What do you need money for?
Are you good at saving money?
Are you a big spender?

Practice asking and answering the questions above with different partners.

Watch out!

Be careful not to make these common mistakes!

I not good at money.	I'm not good with money
It needs much money.	It's expensive.
I don't hold credit card.	I don't have a credit card.

Practice saying these out loud so you can remember them.

Language point

which   *what*   *how*

Which do you prefer, to save money or spend money?

What do you like to buy when you go shopping?

How do you set up an online bank account?

PRACTICE

Write the correct words on the lines below.

1. _____ do you think is better with cake, tea or coffee?

2. _____ did she decide on the charity to give to?

3. _____ do you want in your coffee?

4. _____ investments did he make on the stock market?

5. _____ do you usually use, a credit card or cash?

Conversation strategies

Introducing a new topic

Use this phrase to introduce a new topic or idea.

Oh, before I forget . . .

So I'm saving money to study abroad.

Sounds good. Oh, before I forget, I want to give you something.

Giving a present

Here are some expressions you can use when you give someone a present.

Let me give you this.
I want to give you something.

This is for you.
This is from me and my friends.

Sounds good. Oh, before I forget, I want to give you something.

Oh my gosh! What's this?

It's a piggy bank — to help you save money for your trip.

PRACTICE

Work with a partner. Use the phrases above to practice giving a present. Then add extra information. Use the examples below or your own ideas.

It's for your savings.

It's just a little something.

It's to help you pay for _____

It's a gift card _____

Your ideas: _____

_____

Accepting a present

Here are some common phrases you can use when accepting a gift.

(Oh no.) You shouldn't have!

Thanks so much.

I (really) appreciate it.

It's a piggy bank – to help you save money for your trip.

Oh no. You shouldn't have!

PRACTICE

Work with a partner. Complete the chart below with your own ideas. Then use the expression on pages 26 and 27 and practice conversations in which you give and accept gifts. Follow the steps below.

Gift	Reason for the gift
piggy bank	to help save money for a trip

1. Introduce the topic
2. Give a present
3. Accept the present

TIP   Use the expressions below to react to what your partner says and show surprise. It shows you are interested.
Really?
Oh my gosh!
You're kidding!

Conversation listening

A First listening

Listen to the conversations. How will the speakers spend their money? Circle A or B.

1. **A**    **B**

2. **A**    **B**

3. **A**    **B**

4. **A**    **B**

B Second listening

What do the speakers say about their money situation? Number the items 1–4. One is not used.

_____ wants to save money   _____ is short of money

_____ has a high salary   _____ spends money in a bookstore

_____ saves money by living at home

C Noticing the conversation strategies

Listen for the phrases the speakers use when giving presents. Match the gift they give with the reason they give it.

	Gift	Reason
1.	_____ a card with cash	a) new job
2.	_____ a gift card	b) trip
3.	_____ a book	c) birthday
4.	_____ a piggy bank	d) going-away present

Get ready!

Organize your questions, answers, and vocabulary here to get ready for your *Money* conversation.

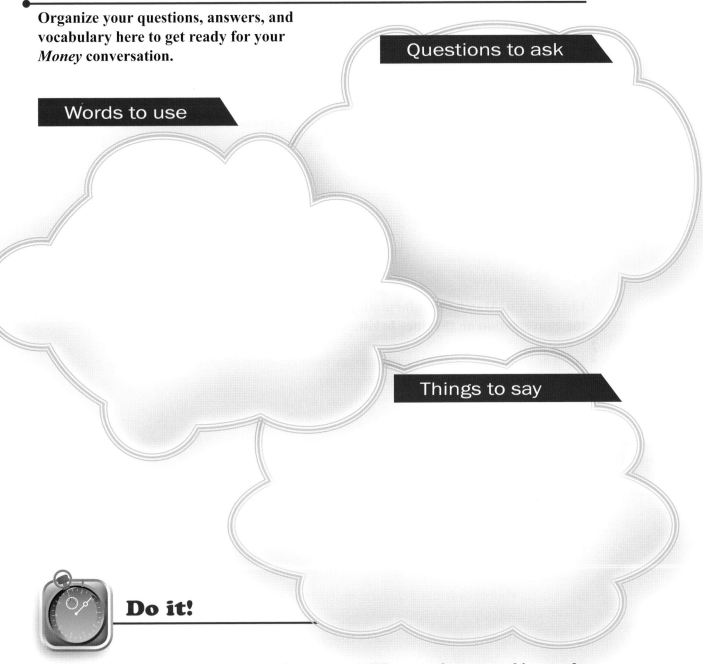

Questions to ask

Words to use

Things to say

Do it!

Practice some timed conversations with partners. When you hear something good, write it on this page after your conversation so you can remember it!

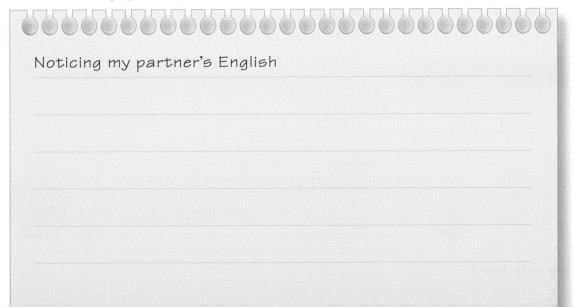

Noticing my partner's English

Real conversations

A Listening

Listen to three conversations about people's spending habits. What do the speakers say they spend money on? Check (✔) the boxes below. You may check more than one box for each conversation.

Category	Conversation 1	Conversation 2	Conversation 3
Entertainment	☐	☐	☐
Makeup	☐	☐	☐
Clothes	☐	☐	☐
Shoes	☐	☐	☐
Food	☐	☐	☐

B Vocabulary

Listen again. Match the information with each conversation. Write the number of the conversation on the lines below.

1. The woman doesn't have any money because she is hopeless at saving. _____
2. The man needs money to pay the rent. _____
3. The woman spends money mostly on herself. _____

Thinking about . . .

Money matters

People have different attitudes toward money. How about you? Read the sentences below. Write A if you agree, D if you disagree, and a question mark (?) if you aren't sure.

1. _____ You should never talk about how much money you make.
2. _____ People only need to earn enough money to live; working to save money is bad.
3. _____ Buying something new in order to make you happy is a dangerous habit.
4. _____ People shouldn't ask others how much something cost.
5. _____ Nothing is more important than money, because money buys everything you need.
6. _____ The more money you have, the happier you are.

PRACTICE

Share your opinions with your partner.

> Money is necessary, but it's not really important. What's important is your family and your health.

> I think so too. Money is useful, but it's not number one.

www.nicetalkingwithyou.com

 Share your opinions with people your age. Listen to Global Voices to hear what English speakers around the world have to say.

Going out

Likes and dislikes

How often do you go out to the places below? Put checks (✔) in the boxes.

Place	Often	Sometimes	Almost never
movie theater			
restaurant			
theme park			
karaoke club			
concert			
shopping mall			
art museum			
park			
night club			

 www.nicetalkingwithyou.com
Share your likes and dislikes with other people like you.

Words and phrases

Check the meaning of these words and phrases. Then use them to do the activities on the next page.

all ages show	classy	feed the animals	pub
arcade games	costume party	get dressed up	roller coaster
backstage pass	cuisine	greenhouse	theater
bowling	dance club	house party	thrill rides
box office	deli	local music scene	young crowd
bring snacks	diner	new movie	watch a show
café	drinks	picnic	
carnival games	exotic	pool hall	

Match it

Match the word on the left with the meaning on the right. Write the letter on the line. Then check your answers with a partner.

1. _____ greenhouse
2. _____ pool hall
3. _____ box office
4. _____ exotic
5. _____ roller coaster
6. _____ classy

a) an amusement park ride with a rail track and steep slopes

b) a place in a theater where people buy tickets

c) stylish and elegant

d) a building where people can play pool

e) a building with clear walls and sides to keep plants warm and protect them

f) something unusual that comes from a place far away

Fill it in

Use the words and phrases on page 31 to complete the sentences. Then check your answers with a partner.

1. Nick is really into the _____ _____ _____. Every Friday night he goes to see live bands.

2. My friend is having a _____ _____ on Saturday night, but I don't know what to wear!

3. Alyssa really loves _____ _____, and she has a million stuffed toys from the crane machines.

4. Mike wants to go see a _____ _____, but Christa wants to talk, so _____ is better.

5. We love going to the petting zoo to _____ _____ _____.

6. Movie theater food is expensive, so Lauren asked me to _____ _____.

7. Andy and Tanya went to a new _____ _____ last weekend. They said it was really fun and full of people.

8. My wife hates _____ _____ _____, so we're just going to stay in and watch old romantic movies.

Put it together

Draw a line to put the sentences together.

1. My friend works for a concert house and

2. I love going to street festivals and

3. On a rainy day I like

4. Tammy doesn't like amusement parks because

5. The weather is beautiful, so

just sitting in a café and drinking coffee.

she hates thrill rides.

let's go to the park and have a picnic.

he got us backstage passes!

playing carnival games.

Listen to check your answers.

Conversation questions

> Where do you like to go?
> What do you like to do?
> Who do you go out with?

Practice asking and answering the questions above with different partners.

Watch out!

Be careful not to make these common mistakes!

✗	✔
~~I like go with my friend.~~	I like going / to go with my friend.
~~We enjoy to play downtown.~~	We enjoy hanging out downtown.
~~I know new restaurant.~~	There's a new restaurant.

Practice saying these out loud so you can remember them.

Language point

Gerund and infinitive: **like, would like, enjoy, love, hate**

My brother **likes playing / to play** arcade games on weekends.

Would you **like to try** the pasta at that restaurant?

The kids really **enjoyed feeding** the animals.

My uncle **loves fishing / to fish** in the summertime.

Sandy **hates watching / to watch** musicals.

PRACTICE

Read the sentences below. Circle the correct form of the verb. Both forms may be correct.

1. Would you like *to go / going* to a dance club on Saturday?

2. I really hate *to eat / eating* at that diner.

3. The young crowd usually enjoy *to hang / hanging* out in the local park.

4. My parents love *to go / going* to the theater.

5. My sister likes *to try / trying* exotic cuisine.

Conversation strategies

Introducing a suggestion

Use the expression below to introduce a suggestion or idea.

(Hey) I have an idea!

I like to go to the park this time of year.

Yeah, me too. I have an idea! Let's go take a walk in the park and take pictures of us with the flowers.

Great idea!

> **TIP** Use the phrase *Me too* to show you share your partner's interests.

Making a specific invitation

Use these phrases to invite someone to do something specific.

**If you have time, let's . . .
If you're not so busy, let's . . .
If you're free, how about . . .**

I have an idea! If you have time on Friday night, let's go to that new club.

Oh cool! I want to check that out.

PRACTICE

Use the expressions above to invite your partner to do something. Add your own ideas to the examples below.

Go out to eat and _____

Check out the new club and _____

Visit a theme park and _____

Go to the zoo and gardens and _____

Go to a concert and _____

Watch a movie and _____

Accepting a specific invitation

Use these expressions to accept an invitation.

> **Sounds good. Sure, I'd love to.**

> **When/Where do you want to meet/go?**

If you're not so busy next weekend, let's go get pizza at that new restaurant.

Sure, I'd love to. When do you want to go?

How about Saturday night?

Declining a specific invitation

It's important to be polite when you decline an invitation. Here are some polite ways to say no to an invitation.

> **Well, that's a great idea, but . . .**

> **Um, I'd love to, but . . .**

> **Well, thanks, but . . .**

If you're free next weekend, how about going to the movies?

Um, I'd love to, but I'm busy next weekend.

Oh, OK. No problem. Some other time?

Yeah, sounds good.

TIP Remember to use *(Oh) That's OK, That's all right, or OK, no problem* after someone declines an invitation. It shows you are not upset.

PRACTICE

Read the excuses below and add two more to the list. Then practice inviting and accepting or declining the invitations with different partners.

I'm busy that weekend.

I have to study.

I already made other plans.

I have to wash my hair.

_____

_____

Conversation listening

A First listening

Listen to the conversations. What kind of places are the speakers talking about?
Circle A or B.

1. A  B

2. A  B

3. A  B

4. A  B

B Second listening

What else do you learn from the speakers? Circle A or B.

1. **A** Some friends are going to another club. **B** The other club is free.

2. **A** The gym has an outdoor exercising area. **B** The friend can get one week's free membership.

3. **A** They are going to meet at 7pm. **B** He has an extra ticket to a game.

4. **A** The golf park manager gave the man tickets. **B** George is the manager of a mini-golf park.

C Noticing the conversation strategies

Listen for the words or phrases the speakers use to respond to the invitations
and decide if they accept or not. Put checks (✔) in the boxes.

Conversation	Does the speaker accept the invitation?	
1.	☐ Yes	☐ No
2.	☐ Yes	☐ No
3.	☐ Yes	☐ No
4.	☐ Yes	☐ No

Get ready!

Organize your questions, answers, and vocabulary here to get ready for your *Going out* conversation.

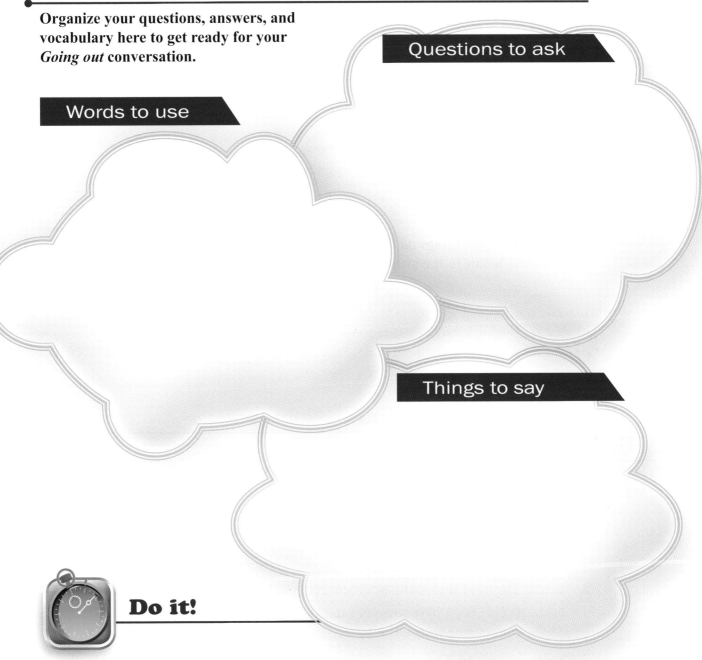

Questions to ask

Words to use

Things to say

Do it!

Practice some timed conversations with partners. When you hear something good, write it on this page after your conversation so you can remember it!

Noticing my partner's English

Real conversations

A Listening

Listen to four conversations about people going out. Decide if the statements are true or false. Write T if they are true and F if they are false.

1. The second woman doesn't like going to nightclubs. _____
2. The woman likes French restaurants. _____
3. The women enjoy shopping and karaoke. _____
4. The man buys a lot of things for his girlfriend. _____

B Vocabulary

Listen again. What things do the speakers say they do when they go out? Number the activities below in the order you hear them.

a) _____ eating out
b) _____ shopping
c) _____ singing karaoke
d) _____ going to amusement parks

e) _____ going to night clubs
f) _____ going to the beach
g) _____ watching movies

Thinking about . . .

Going out

Why do people go out? Read the sentences below. Write A if you agree and D if you disagree.

1. _____ It's important to go out because staying at home all the time is mentally unhealthy.
2. _____ Society encourages people to go out so that they will spend their money.
3. _____ The most important aspect of going out is interacting with other people.
4. _____ People don't have to go out to have fun; there's nothing wrong with entertaining yourself at home.
5. _____ Going out widens your worldview and brings you experiences you could never get if you stayed home.

 PRACTICE

Share your opinions with your partner.

> I don't think it's strange to stay at home a lot. These days, we can be social without going out.

> Maybe, but going out makes you interact with people, and that's so important!

www.nicetalkingwithyou.com

Share your opinions with people your age. Listen to Global Voices to hear what English speakers around the world have to say.

Fashion

Likes and dislikes

How much do you like fashion? What kind of fashion do you like? Read the statements below. Put checks (✔) in the boxes below.

I like . . .

	😃	🙂	😐	🙁	☹️
reading fashion magazines.					
getting new hairstyles.					
trying different styles of clothing.					
piercings and tattoos.					
jewelry on men.					

www.nicetalkingwithyou.com
Share your likes and dislikes with other people like you.

Words and phrases

Check the meaning of these words and phrases. Then use them to do the activities on the next page.

beautician	fashion victim	gothic	metrosexual	stylist
bohemian	flashy	hairdresser	modestly	tacky
clothing	(un)flattering	hairstyle	plaid	trendsetter
designer	frumpy	hip-hop	preppy	uniform
couture	geek chic	label	punk rock	
eccentric	girly	lace	salon	
fashion blogger	glam	manicure	sporty	

Match it

Match the word on the left with the meaning on the right. Write the letter on the line. Then check your answers with a partner.

1. _____ couture
2. _____ clothing designer
3. _____ beautician
4. _____ uniform
5. _____ trendsetter
6. _____ preppy

a) a person who gives beauty treatments
b) neat and traditional style of dress
c) someone who starts new fashions
d) high-fashion, custom-made clothing
e) a set of clothing required by a job or school
f) an artist who imagines and creates clothes

Fill it in

Use the words and phrases on page 39 to complete the sentences. Then check your answers with a partner.

1. Camille is a _____ _____, but she writes about more than just the clothes and designers she likes.

2. My friend wears very _____ clothes and that fits her laid-back, _____ lifestyle.

3. Kyle always tries to wear the cool new thing, but he ends up looking like a _____.

4. She really does a good job of dressing _____ without looking _____.

5. I don't like _____ style much, but the dark makeup and dramatic clothes suit him well.

6. My sister's _____ went too far. She really chopped her bangs too short.

7. All she cares about is the _____ on her clothes.

8. Felicia's clothes are so _____; everything she owns is covered in _____ and ribbons.

Put it together

Draw a line to put the sentences together.

1. Ben is a metrosexual. He gets

2. Jennifer is really into punk rock, so she owns

3. Maria is really good at accessorizing, and she

4. Kat really likes hip-hop music, but she doesn't

5. Naomi likes guys who wear glasses, so she says

wants to be a stylist.

her type is geek chic.

a lot of black and plaid clothes.

a manicure once a month.

wear the clothes.

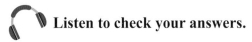 **Listen to check your answers.**

Conversation questions

> What's your style?
>
> What style is popular?
>
> What style do you think is interesting?
>
> What's a style you don't like?

Practice asking and answering the questions above with different partners.

Watch out!

Be careful not to make these common mistakes!

✗	✔
~~I like brand.~~	I like famous brands.
~~I don't care style.~~	I don't care about style. / I'm not interested in style.
~~She's beautician.~~	She's a beautician.

Practice saying these out loud so you can remember them!

Language point

Adjectives

I'm not a fan of **dark** clothing styles.

Many girls like a **casual** look.

She doesn't usually wear **flashy** clothes.

Adverbs

I like guys who dress **nicely**.

She **mostly** wears bright, vivid colors.

Dressing **fashionably** often takes money.

PRACTICE

Read the sentences below. Circle the correct form of the words in italics.

1. My brother says he *usual / usually* prefers a sporty look.

2. The singer in the concert wore very *tacky / tackily* costumes.

3. He is well known for his *eccentric / eccentrically* styles.

4. I like guys who dress *casual / casually*.

5. She's a clothing designer but always wears *preppy / preppily* clothes.

Conversation strategies

Changing the focus of a topic

You can use this expression to introduce a new topic or change the focus of a topic.

By the way . . .

So yes, I'm into fashion and style. By the way, that's a nice watch.

Thanks!

Giving a compliment

Here are some adjectives you can use to pay a compliment.

Nice / cool / cute . . .

I like casual style clothing. By the way, nice necklace!

This? Thanks. It was really cheap!

PRACTICE

Add two more items to the list below. Then use *By the way* to give compliments to different partners.

shirt/top

glasses

hairstyle

shoes

_____

_____

By the way, cute top!

Thanks!

Asking for an explanation

Use this phrase when you don't understand and you need an explanation.

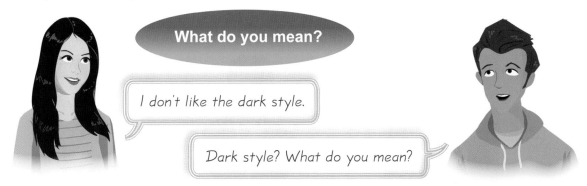

What do you mean?

I don't like the dark style.

Dark style? What do you mean?

Beginning an explanation

Use these phrases to help you explain something.

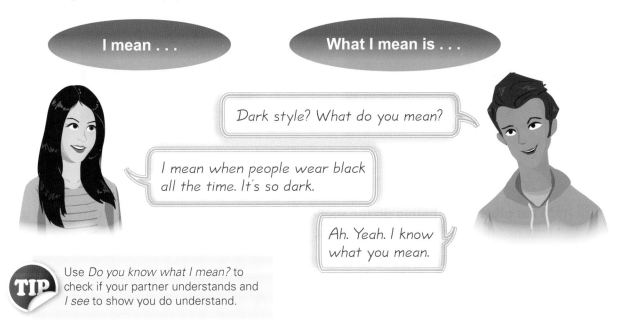

I mean . . .

What I mean is . . .

Dark style? What do you mean?

I mean when people wear black all the time. It's so dark.

Ah. Yeah. I know what you mean.

TIP Use *Do you know what I mean?* to check if your partner understands and *I see* to show you do understand.

PRACTICE

Write three sentences about fashion that will make your partner say *What do you mean?* Then use *I mean* to begin your explanation.

For example:

A: I don't understand tattoos.

B: What do you mean?

A: I mean, why do people change their bodies like that? I just couldn't do it.

1. _____

2. _____

3. _____

Conversation listening

A First listening

Listen to the conversations. What fashion styles are the speakers talking about? Number the photos in the order you hear about them. One is not used.

☐    ☐    ☐

☐    ☐

B Second listening

What other information do the speakers share? Decide if the statements below are true or false. Write T if they are true and F if they are false.

1. **A** The dress was a present from her mother. _____
   B They are both tall and thin. _____

2. **A** He likes her shoes. _____
   B Her shoes weren't cheap. _____

3. **A** He has a piercing and pink hair. _____
   B His girlfriend likes his new style. _____

4. **A** Her dress is new. _____
   B He thinks she looked great in her dress. _____

C Noticing the conversation strategies

Listen for the expression *I mean* and the phrase that follows it in each conversation. Number the expressions below in the order you hear them.

a) the flashy look-at-me style _____
b) the girls who are all in black _____
c) couture – the beautiful fashion-model look _____
d) the polo shirts and the expensive brand-name sneakers _____

Get ready!

Organize your questions, answers, and vocabulary here to get ready for your *Fashion* conversation.

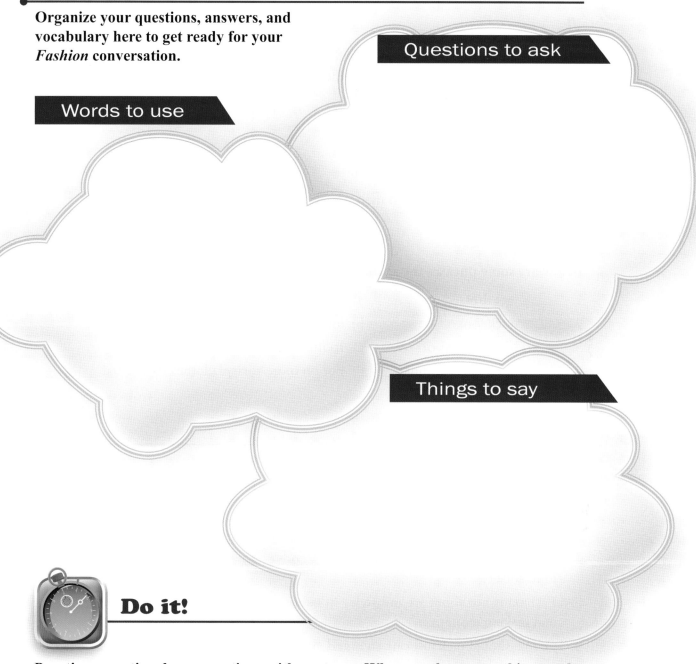

Words to use

Questions to ask

Things to say

Do it!

Practice some timed conversations with partners. When you hear something good, write it on this page after your conversation so you can remember it!

Noticing my partner's English

Real conversations

A Listening

Listen to four conversations about fashion styles. You will hear the speakers talking about their likes and dislikes. Number the items below in the order you hear about them.

a) _____ girls with a lot of makeup

b) _____ black clothes

c) _____ casual style

d) _____ baggy pants

e) _____ feminine fashion on men

B Vocabulary

Below are some phrases the speakers use. Match them to their meanings.

1. _____ get dressed up   a) it's unattractive

2. _____ jock look   b) look too pale

3. _____ that's a turn-off   c) football player style

4. _____ look like a zombie   d) put on more formal clothes than usual

Thinking about . . .

The point of fashion

What's so important about fashion? Read the sentences below. Write 1–5. (1 means you strongly agree; 5 means you strongly disagree.)

1. People who always follow the latest fashions have no imagination. _____

2. It's important to keep up with fashion trends so that you can fit in to society. _____

3. Fashion is not about art and style – it's about selling clothes and making money. _____

4. People should pick just one style and stay with it; they shouldn't change styles so often. _____

5. Creativity, not marketing, drives the fashion world. _____

 PRACTICE

Share your opinions with your partner.

> I think fashion is great because it lets you be creative and imaginative. What do you think?

> I don't agree. I think most people just copy other styles, and that's not creative.

www.nicetalkingwithyou.com
Share your opinions with people your age. Listen to Global Voices
to hear what English speakers around the world have to say.

Learning

Likes and dislikes

We all enjoy learning new things. What kinds of learning are most interesting to you? Write 1–5 below. (1= you like it the most; 5 = you like it the least)

Learning …

to make something (e.g., clothes, a table, food) _____

to get more knowledge (e.g., current events, global issues) _____

to make your body stronger, better, fitter _____

to create something artistic (e.g., painting, writing) _____

to develop a skill (e.g., language, music) _____

 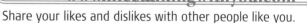 **www.nicetalkingwithyou.com**

Share your likes and dislikes with other people like you.

Words and phrases

Check the meaning of these words and phrases. Then use them to do the activities on the next page.

acting	flower arranging	painting
ballet	gardening	piano instructor
ballroom dance	golf	pottery
computer software	guitar	scrapbooking
cooking class	home improvement	tailor
culinary arts school	horseback riding	voice lessons
do-it-yourself (DIY)	knit	workshop
enrichment course	music appreciation	yoga
etiquette	nutrition	
first aid	obedience training	

Match it

Match the word on the left with the meaning on the right. Write the letter on the line. Then check your answers with a partner.

1. _____ etiquette
2. _____ pottery
3. _____ tailor
4. _____ nutrition
5. _____ scrapbooking
6. _____ voice lessons

a) the science of food and health
b) someone who makes or repairs clothes
c) pasting photos and other decorations into an album
d) instruction on controlling your voice and singing
e) the art of shaping clay into objects
f) manners or rules of behavior

Fill it in

Use the words and phrases on page 47 to complete the sentences. Then check your answers with a partner.

1. I took a _____ _____ class and learned how to do the waltz and the tango.

2. Lee wants to become a pastry chef, so she is looking for a good _____ _____ _____.

3. Dad retired last year, but he is taking an _____ _____ at the community college to keep busy.

4. Miki is taking a _____ _____ course. She's learning how to clean and bandage wounds.

5. My grandma loves _____, but when it gets too cold for her to grow anything she _____.

6. I ran into my neighbor at the _____ _____ store. He is remodeling his kitchen.

7. Janet got a new puppy, so she is taking it to _____ _____ every week.

8. My brother can't draw very well, but he loves art and wants to study _____.

Put it together

Draw a line to put the sentences together.

1. Nicole is doing an acting workshop,
2. He won't do ballet
3. Brad is living on his own,
4. David loves to go surfing,
5. Her neighbor plays the guitar really loud,

so he's taking a cooking class.

so he's gotten really tanned this summer.

so she wants to move out.

so she's busy this weekend.

because he thinks it's girly.

 **Listen to check your answers.**

Conversation questions

> What are you interested in?
>
> Are you studying anything these days?
>
> What kind of things do you like learning about?

Practice asking and answering the questions above with different partners.

Watch out!

Be careful not to make these common mistakes.

✗	✔
I have many interesting things.	I'm interested in many things.
I don't like study.	I don't like to study. / I don't like studying.
I want learn the guitar.	I want to learn the guitar.

Practice saying these out loud so you can remember them!

Language point

lend

Could you *lend* me your pencil?

I hope she'll *lend* that book to me when she's finished reading it.

borrow

Can I *borrow* that till next week?

Do you think I could *borrow* 10 dollars and pay you back on Monday?

PRACTICE

Complete the sentences. Write *lend* or *borrow* on the lines below.

1. I'll _____ you my tennis racket if you can give it back on Monday.

2. She wanted to _____ my MP3 player to use in the gym.

3. Do you really want to _____ my car this weekend?

4. My advice is never to _____ money to people you don't know well.

5. Would it be OK to _____ your book on first aid for a few days?

Conversation strategies

Preparing the listener

Use this phrase before making a request. It helps prepare the listener for what you are going to say next.

(Um) You know what?

Wow. You have the Zoombah workout DVD.

Yeah.

You know what? I would love to try Zoombah.

Asking permission

Use these phrases to ask to borrow something.

Could/Can I borrow this?

Do you think I could borrow this?

Would it be OK if I borrowed this?

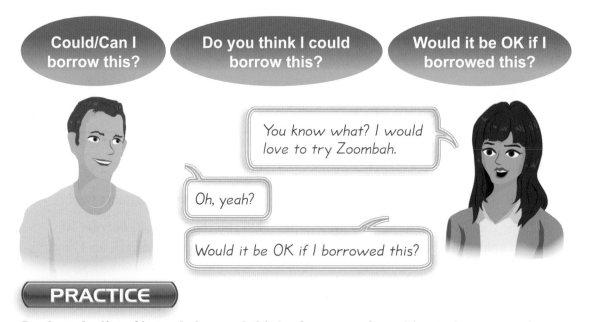

You know what? I would love to try Zoombah.

Oh, yeah?

Would it be OK if I borrowed this?

PRACTICE

Look at the list of items below and think of a reason for asking to borrow each. Write on the lines. Then add two more items of your own. Use the expressions above to practice asking your partner if you can borrow the items.

Item	Reason for borrowing
your phone	_____
your watch	_____
your textbook	_____
Your ideas: _____	_____
_____	_____

Making a promise

Here are some expressions you can use to make a promise.

> I'll give it back next week.

> I won't lose it, I promise.

> (I promise) I'll take good care of it.

> Do you think I could borrow this? I promise I'll give it back next week.

Giving permission

Use these phrases to give someone permission to do something.

> Sure, go ahead.

> Be my guest.

> Yeah, no problem.

> Would it be OK if I borrowed this? I'll give it back next week.

> Sure, go ahead. Just don't lose it!

PRACTICE

Work with a partner. Follow the steps below and use all the strategies on pages 50 and 51 to practice a complete conversation.

1. Prepare the listener

2. Ask permission

3. Make a promise

4. Give permission

Conversation listening

A First listening

What do the speakers do in their free time? What activities do they talk about the most? Circle A or B.

1. A B

3. A B

2. A B

4. A  B

B Second listening

Why do the people want to borrow the items? Put checks (✔) in the boxes.

1. The woman wants to learn . . .
   - ☐ more about the man.
   - ☐ how to use iTunes.
   - ☐ about how humans think.

2. The man wants to learn to play . . .
   - ☐ his grandfather's music.
   - ☐ some famous songs.
   - ☐ some music he borrowed.

3. The man wants to . . .
   - ☐ start teaching.
   - ☐ understand more about money.
   - ☐ make a documentary.

4. The woman wants to . . .
   - ☐ learn how to relax.
   - ☐ sell her bike.
   - ☐ rent a room.

C Noticing the conversation strategies

What promises do the speakers make about the items? Number them in the order you hear them. One is not used.

The speaker promises . . .

a) _____ not to lose it.

b) _____ to return it next week.

c) _____ not to break it.

d) _____ to return it soon.

e) _____ to take good care of it.

Get ready!

Organize your questions, answers, and vocabulary here to get ready for your *Learning* conversation.

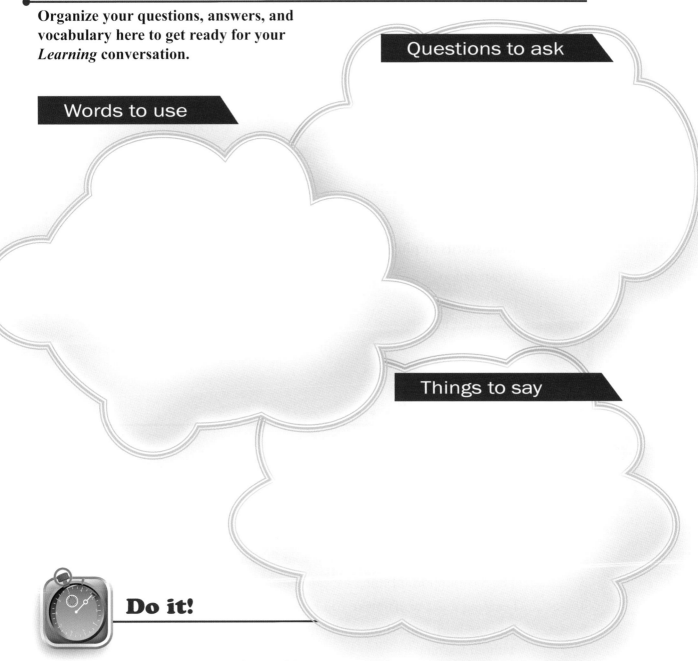

Questions to ask

Words to use

Things to say

Do it!

Practice some timed conversations with partners. When you hear something good, write it on this page after your conversation so you can remember it!

Noticing my partner's English

Real conversations

A Listening

Listen to six short conversations in which people talk about what they are learning. What things are they learning? Number the topics in the order you hear them.

a) ＿＿＿ American culture

b) ＿＿＿ yoga

c) ＿＿＿ German

d) ＿＿＿ Chinese

e) ＿＿＿ cooking

f) ＿＿＿ astronomy

g) ＿＿＿ sewing

B Vocabulary

Below are some words or phrases the speakers use. Match them to their meanings.

1. ＿＿＿ constellation

2. ＿＿＿ pick up

3. ＿＿＿ jump right into it

4. ＿＿＿ pose

a) learn

b) start something immediately; do your best

c) the way you stand or sit

d) group of stars that forms a pattern

Thinking about . . .

Why keep learning?

What is your attitude toward learning? Read the sentences below. Write A if you agree and D if you disagree.

1. ＿＿＿ People shouldn't always be trying to learn new things; they should be satisfied with the way they are.

2. ＿＿＿ Learning is the key to improving your life and improving the world.

3. ＿＿＿ The most important thing we can learn is how to learn.

4. ＿＿＿ Learning more won't make you happy, but it will make you smarter.

5. ＿＿＿ You can learn something without studying it and study something without learning it.

6. ＿＿＿ People love learning because humans are naturally curious.

 PRACTICE

Share your opinions with your partner.

> A lot of people are afraid to learn new things. I guess it's because they think learning and studying are the same thing.

> Right. People don't know that learning can be so much fun.

www.nicetalkingwithyou.com

Share your opinions with people your age. Listen to Global Voices to hear what English speakers around the world have to say.

Review 1

 # Conversation strategies

Unit 1

Excuse me . . .

Wow, long time no see! / It's been a while. / a long time. / ages.

How are things? / How have you been?

Anyway, I guess I should go. / Well, I better get going.

Nice talking with you. / Great seeing you again.

Unit 2

Well you know . . .

You should come over sometime. / when you're free. / when you're not too busy.

I'd love to/that. / That would be great. / Good idea! / Sounds great.

Unit 3

Oh, before I forget . . .

Let me give you this. / I want to give you something. / This is for you. / This is from me and my friends.

You shouldn't have! / Thanks so much. / I (really) appreciate it.

Unit 4

I have an idea!

If you have time, let's . . . / If you're not so busy, let's . . . / If you're free, how about . . .

Sounds good. / Sure, I'd love to. When/Where do you want to meet/go?

Well, that's a great idea, but . . . / Um, I'd love to, but . . . / Well, thanks, but . . .

Unit 5

By the way . . .

Nice / cool / cute . . .

What do you mean?

I mean . . . / What I mean is . . .

Unit 6

You know what?

Could/Can I borrow this? / Do you think I could borrow this? / Would it be OK if I borrowed this?

I'll give it back next week. / I won't lose it, I promise. / I'll take good care of it.

Sure, go ahead. / Be my guest. / Yeah, no problem.

55

A. **Review the conversation strategy expressions on page 55. Choose appropriate expressions for each of the four situations below and write them on the lines. Use your own ideas to make notes about each situation.**

Situation 1: Inviting someone to come to your home

Person A: _____

Person B (response): _____

Notes: _____

Situation 2: Giving a present to someone

Person A: _____

Person B (response): _____

Notes: _____

Situation 3: Giving a compliment

Person A: _____

Person B (response): _____

Notes: _____

Situation 4: Asking to borrow something and promising to give it back

Person A: _____

Person B (response): _____

Notes: _____

B. **Work with a partner. Take turns being A and B and practice having conversations for each situation. Try not to look at the book when you speak to your partner.**

LISTENING PRACTICE I

A. **Listen to the four conversations. Match the photos to the conversations. Write the number of the conversation in the box. One photo is not used.**

B. **Listen again. Which conversation strategies do the speakers use? Write the conversation number in the boxes below. One is not used.**

Strategy	Conversation
Asking for an explanation	_____
Asking to borrow something	_____
Giving a compliment	_____
Giving a present	_____
Making an invitation	_____

SPEAKING PRACTICE 2

Review the topics you covered in Units 1 to 6. Choose three from the list below and check (✔) the boxes.

Unit	Topic
☐ Long time no see	meeting an old friend
☐ My place	your home and neighborhood; inviting people over
☐ Money	money; giving and accepting gifts
☐ Going out	places to go to for entertainment; inviting people to do things
☐ Fashion	fashion styles; giving compliments
☐ Learning	different kinds of learning; asking to borrow things

Practice having conversations about your topics with different partners. Use the expressions below to link your ideas and sentences.

Excuse me . . .   Well you know . . .   Oh, before I forget . . .

(Hey) I have an idea!   By the way . . .   (Um) You know what?

LISTENING PRACTICE 2

A. You will hear three conversations in which one speaker invites the other to do something. Do they accept the invitation? Write Yes or No on the lines below.

Conversation	Invitation accepted?
1.	_____
2.	_____
3.	_____

B. Listen again. The speakers use the expressions below to introduce their suggestions. Match the expressions to the invitations. Write the number on the lines. One is not used.

Conversation	Invitation	Expression
1.	To hear a talk	_____ *Oh, before I forget*
2.	To have a party	_____ *Well you know*
3.	To go to a park	_____ *By the way*
		_____ *I have an idea!*

Experience abroad

Likes and dislikes

Would you like to study or live abroad? Read the statements below. Write A if you agree and D if you disagree.

_____ I'd like to go overseas on a visit, but I could never live abroad.

_____ I'd like to live abroad for a while and study something.

_____ If I had the chance, I would work abroad.

_____ If I lived abroad, I would definitely get a roommate.

_____ I couldn't live abroad forever. I would return to my home country
to live someday.

www.nicetalkingwithyou.com

Share your likes and dislikes with other people like you.

Words and phrases

Check the meaning of these words and phrases. Then use them to do the activities on the next page.

adventure	exchange program	interdependence	perspectives
beliefs	field trip	international	region
broaden	firsthand	interpreter	traditions
communicate	foreign language	make friends	translator
cultural values	global society	native	view of the world
diverse	homestay	offend	way of life
embrace	(be) immersed in	opportunity	world religions

Match it

Match the word on the left with the meaning on the right. Write the letter on the line. Then check your answers with a partner.

1. _____ field trip
2. _____ homestay
3. _____ firsthand
4. _____ interdependence
5. _____ native
6. _____ region

a) person born in a particular place
b) unable to exist without each other
c) an area of a country or the world
d) direct personal experience
e) an outing by a school group to study something
f) living in someone else's home in a foreign country

Fill it in

Use the words and phrases on page 59 to complete the sentences. Then check your answers with a partner.

1. The best way to learn a _____ _____ is to be _____ _____ a culture in which it is spoken.

2. Alastair studies _____ _____ because he wants to understand people with different _____.

3. Jeff went on a foreign _____ _____ to Thailand because he was looking for an _____.

4. Before you visit a country, you should study the local _____ _____, so you don't accidentally _____ people.

5. Michael is really good at looking at a problem from different _____.

6. Learning another language helped Jin to _____ better in his native language.

7. Her mom told her that a trip to Japan would really broaden her _____ _____ _____ _____.

8. Studying abroad allows you to _____ _____ with a _____ group of people.

Put it together

Draw a line to complete the sentences.

1. During her homestay, she
2. Noah studies Spanish so he
3. Su-Wei is really good with languages and
4. She likes to dress in traditional clothes
5. My brother loves to travel, and he

so that she can embrace her culture.

never misses an opportunity to see a new place.

learned a lot about the local traditions.

wants to be an interpreter.

can be a participant in global society.

Listen to check your answers.

Conversation questions

Where would you like to live or study abroad?

Why do you want to go there?

What do you want to do there?

Practice asking and answering the questions above with different partners.

Watch out!

Be careful not to make these common mistakes.

✘	✔
~~I want to go to there because . . .~~	I want to go there because . . .
~~I want study special thing.~~	I want to study something special.
~~It's a safety place.~~	It's a safe place.

Practice saying these out loud so you can remember them!

Language point

for

I lived abroad **_for_** one year.

You studied in Australia **_for_** a while, didn't you?

since

We haven't been abroad **_since_** 2007.

I haven't spoken English **_since_** I came back two weeks ago.

PRACTICE

Complete the statements below. Write _for_ or _since_ on the lines below.

1. I'd like to go abroad _____ a few years to get a different experience.

2. _____ she came back from her homestay she has wanted to become a translator.

3. He's been immersed in his studies _____ this morning.

4. Kim's been interested in international opportunities _____ the last couple of years.

5. They have lived overseas _____ 2001.

Conversation strategies

Introducing a request

Use this expression to introduce a request or question.

Can/Could I ask you something?

Can I ask you something?

Sure, what is it?

Asking for advice

Use these phrases to begin your request for advice.

I need some advice about . . .

I could really use your advice/help.

Can I get your advice on something?

Sure, what is it?

I need some advice about what to study.

PRACTICE

Look at the list of topics below. For each one, think of something you could ask advice about. Write them on the lines.

Topic	Advice about
Health	*what food or drink to eat*
Study	*what course . . .*
Gifts	
Going out	
Shopping	

Work with a partner. Use the examples above to practice asking for advice.

Giving advice

Use phrases like these to start your advice.

Why don't you . . .

Maybe you should . . .

I think you should . . .

I need some advice about what to study.

Why don't you take a class in psychology? That's really interesting.

That sounds like a good idea. Thanks!

PRACTICE

Work with a partner. One is Student A, the other is Student B. Read the points below about studying or living overseas. Write two more points to ask for advice about on the lines.

Student A

I need some advice about . . .

• which country to go to

• where to live: in a dorm or with a family

• where to live: in the city or the country

• _____

Student B

I need some advice about . . .

• what to study abroad

• how long I should stay

• what to take abroad with me

• _____

Use the points above and the strategies on pages 62 and 63. Practice asking for advice and giving advice with your partner, like in the example below.

A: *Can I ask you something?*

B: *Sure, what is it?*

A: *I could really use your advice. I want to study English abroad, but I'm not sure which country to go to.*

B: *Why don't you go to New Zealand? I heard there are lots of good schools and it's really beautiful.*

A: *I'll check that out. Thanks!*

Conversation listening

A First listening

Listen to the conversations. Which places do the speakers choose for their international experience? Circle A or B.

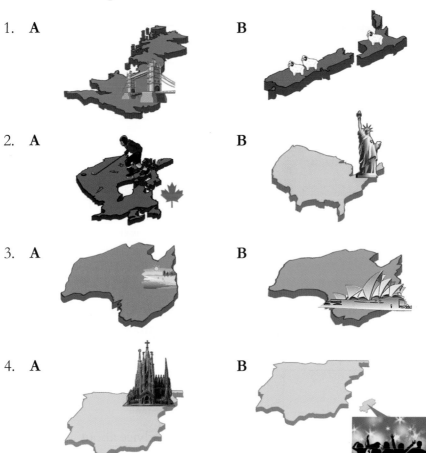

1. A   B

2. A   B

3. A   B

4. A   B

B Second listening

What are the speakers asking advice about? Number the points below in the order you hear about them. One is not used.

a) _____ the quality of the study program

b) _____ serious study or having fun

c) _____ personal safety

d) _____ doing a homestay or staying at a dorm

e) _____ the cost of living abroad

C Noticing the conversation strategies

Listen for the expressions the speakers use to ask for advice and number them in the order you hear them.

a) _____ I could use your help.

b) _____ I could really use your advice.

c) _____ Can I ask you something?

d) _____ Can I get your advice on something?

Get ready!

Organize your questions, answers, and vocabulary here to get ready for your *Experience abroad* conversation.

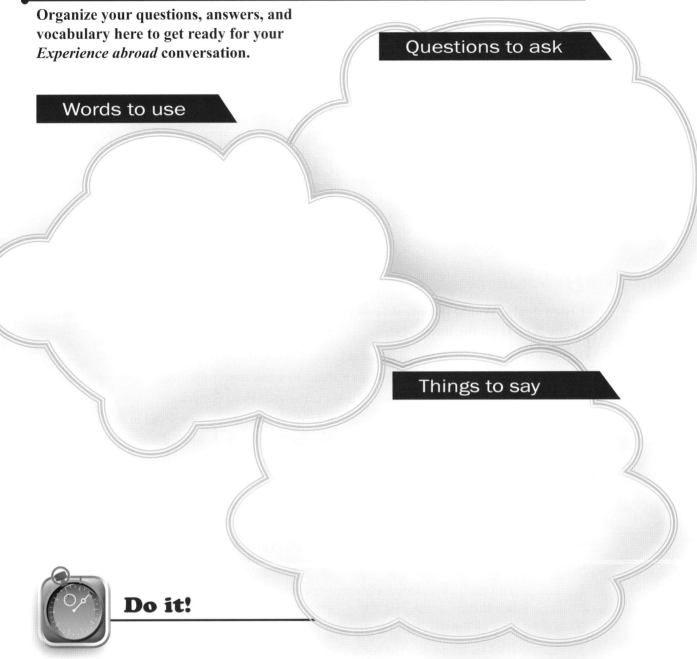

Words to use

Questions to ask

Things to say

Do it!

Practice some timed conversations with partners. When you hear something good, write it on this page after your conversation so you can remember it!

Noticing my partner's English

Real conversations

A Listening

Listen to five short conversations about living abroad. You will hear the speakers talk about three countries. Match the countries with the reasons they give for wanting to go there. Put checks (✔) in the boxes.

	America	England	France
a) To learn about university life	☐	☐	☐
b) To listen to the local accent.	☐	☐	☐
c) To study agriculture	☐	☐	☐
d) To study design	☐	☐	☐
e) To try the food	☐	☐	☐

B Vocabulary

Listen again. Would the speakers agree (A) or disagree (D) with these statements? Write A or D on the lines.

1. First speaker   It would be great to live abroad, in a large house with a pool.   _____
2. Second speaker   It's easier to go abroad to work than to study.   _____
3. First speaker   It's cheaper to live in Australia than America.   _____
4. Second speaker   It's easy to understand British accents if you've lived in the US.   _____
5. Second speaker   A lot of towns in England are really beautiful.   _____

Thinking about . . .

Why live abroad?

Read the opinions below about living abroad. Write A if you agree and D if you disagree.

1. _____ You can't experience a foreign country fully just by visiting it – you have to live there.
2. _____ Living abroad changes the way you look at the world.
3. _____ It's OK to go abroad for a short time, but people shouldn't work abroad. They should stay and support their home country.
4. _____ The most important part of living abroad is meeting new people and learning about their way of thinking.
5. _____ It's strange to want to live in a foreign country.

PRACTICE

Share your opinions with your partner.

> I think it's true that living abroad changes your worldview, but an overseas vacation is enough for me!

> I know what you mean. Most people want to travel abroad, but they don't want to live there!

www.nicetalkingwithyou.com

Share your opinions with people your age. Listen to Global Voices to hear what English speakers around the world have to say.

Health

Likes and dislikes

What things do you do to keep healthy? How often do you do them? Put checks (✔) in the boxes below.

	Often	Sometimes	Almost never
Do exercise			
Do yoga			
Drink water and tea			
Eat healthy food			
Get at least seven hours of sleep			
Meditate			
Take vitamins			

www.nicetalkingwithyou.com

Share your likes and dislikes with other people like you.

Words and phrases

Check the meaning of these words and phrases. Then use them to do the activities on the next page.

active	checkup	in moderation	meditation	take the stairs
added sugar	diabetes	jogging	obesity	time management
asthma	fiber	kickboxing	organic food	vitamins
balanced diet	health club	laughter	pilates	weightlifting
belly dancing	heart disease	low fat	protein shake	work out
caffeine	ingredients	marathon	sleep deprived	

Match it

Match the word on the left with the meaning on the right. Write the letter on the line. Then check your answers with a partner.

1. _____ asthma
2. _____ organic
3. _____ caffeine
4. _____ ingredients
5. _____ obesity
6. _____ vitamins

a) chemical in coffee, tea, and cola that can keep you awake
b) natural substances in food that are needed for good health
c) condition of being medically overweight
d) illness where a person has trouble breathing
e) grown and produced without man-made chemicals
f) the items used to make something

Fill it in

Use the words and phrases on page 67 to complete the sentences. Then check your answers with a partner.

1. Mei tries hard to stay _____, but she doesn't have time to go to the gym.

2. She is careful about what she eats, so she even checks the label on fruit juice for _____ _____.

3. I think a _____ _____ is the most important thing for your health, but I've heard that _____ is the best medicine.

4. My best friend doesn't really like exercising or sports, but she stays fit by _____ _____.

5. It's too cold outside to go _____, so Sachi joined a _____ _____ to work out during the winter.

6. My grandmother says that you can eat whatever you want, as long as it's _____ _____.

7. Kelsey gets really worried about handling both work and school, so she took a class in _____ _____.

8. Around finals week, most of the students on campus start to look really _____ _____.

Put it together

Draw a line to put the sentences together.

1. Rachel wants to run a marathon,
2. She loves kickboxing
3. David started doing yoga,
4. My dad is too busy to work out,
5. Even though diabetes runs in Jessica's family,

she eats a lot of sweets.

and he finds meditation really relaxing.

because it takes her mind off her problems.

so she goes to the health club and works out every day.

so he just takes the stairs whenever he can.

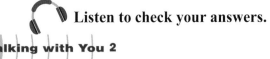 **Listen to check your answers.**

Conversation questions

> What do you do to keep healthy?
>
> Do you ever exercise / work out / meditate?
>
> How do you deal with stress?

Practice asking and answering the questions above with different partners.

Watch out!

Be careful not to make these common mistakes!

✗	✔
~~What do you do to keep your health?~~	What do you do to keep healthy?
~~XXXXXX is good for health.~~	XXXXXX is good for your health.
~~I want to lose my weight.~~	I want to lose weight.

Practice saying these out loud so you can remember them!

Language point

because

He works out three or four times a week ***because*** he wants to lose weight.

I stopped drinking coffee in the evening ***because*** I couldn't sleep.

so

Jody wants to stay healthy ***so*** she eats a lot of fruits and vegetables.

She really wants to win the competition ***so*** she's training every day for three hours.

PRACTICE

Read the statements below. Circle *because* or *so*.

1. She always buys organic food *because* / *so* she read it is much healthier.

2. Tom doesn't eat fast food these days *because* / *so* his doctor told him he was overweight.

3. My sister learned that too much red meat is bad for you *because* / *so* she only has steak once a month.

4. I never go to the gym *because* / *so* I think it's boring and I'm too busy.

5. Jim wanted to learn how to be more efficient at work *because* / *so* he took a course in time management.

Conversation strategies

Introducing a related comment

Use this phrase to introduce a new comment related to the one before.

Speaking of . . .

I know I should really go exercise at a gym.

Speaking of gym exercise, I have a discount coupon.

Making an offer

Use these phrases to offer something to someone.

Would you like it?

Can/Could you use it?

Speaking of gym exercise, I have a discount coupon. Would you like it?

A discount coupon? Hmm . . .

PRACTICE

Draw lines to connect the topics on the left with the offer that best matches it. Write two of your own original topics and offers. Then use the strategies above to practice making offers to your partner.

Topic	Offer
energy drinks	electric back massager
healthy food	a free lotion sample
stress	a bite of my apple.
eating fruit	new vitamin drink
smooth skin	gift card for a free healthy-cooking lesson
_____	_____
_____	_____

Declining an offer

When you decline someone's offer, it's important to be polite. Use these phrases.

> Thanks very much,
> but that's OK.

> That's so nice of you,
> but I'll pass.

> That's OK.
> But I appreciate the offer.

A discount coupon? Hmm. Thanks very much, but that's OK.

Ah, all right. No problem.

PRACTICE

Work with a new partner. Use the strategies on pages 70 and 71 to make and decline offers. You can use the examples on page 70 or write new ideas on the lines below.

Topic	Offer
Drink	_____
Food	_____
Exercise	_____
Stress	_____
Your ideas: _____	_____
_____	_____

Conversation listening

A First listening

Listen to the conversations. Number the pictures in the order you hear about them. One is not used.

☐

☐

☐

☐

☐

B Second listening

What are the speakers offering? Circle A or B.

1. **A** a discount coupon   **B** a free ticket

2. **A** a bottle of water   **B** some cold medicine

3. **A** an alarm clock   **B** a sleep-aid gadget

4. **A** discount membership   **B** a free pass

C Noticing the conversation strategies

Listen for the responses and decide if the offer is accepted or rejected. Put checks (✔) in the boxes.

| | The offer is . . . | |
Conversation	accepted	rejected
1.	☐	☐
2.	☐	☐
3.	☐	☐
4.	☐	☐

Get ready!

Organize your questions, answers, and vocabulary here to get ready for your *Health* conversation.

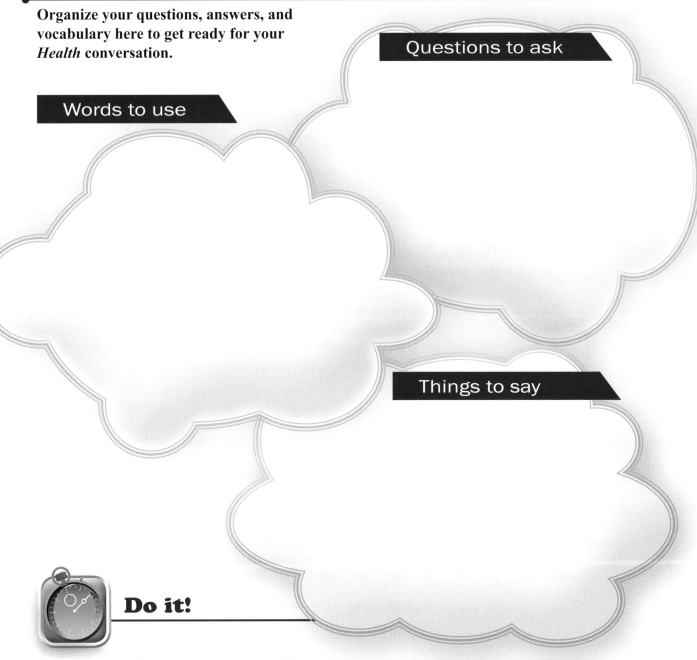

Questions to ask

Words to use

Things to say

Do it!

Practice some timed conversations with partners. When you hear something good, write it on this page after your conversation so you can remember it!

Noticing my partner's English

Real conversations

A Listening

Listen to three short conversations in which people talk about health. Answer the questions below. Circle Y for Yes, N for No, and ? if you aren't sure.

Does the speaker . . .	do exercise?	eat healthily?	have stress?
1. Second speaker	Y / N / ?	Y / N / ?	Y / N / ?
2. Woman	Y / N / ?	Y / N / ?	Y / N / ?
3. First speaker	Y / N / ?	Y / N / ?	Y / N / ?

B Vocabulary

Listen again. Decide if the statements below are true or false. Write T if they are true and F if they are false.

1.	Second speaker	He relieves stress by singing.	_____
2.	Woman	She takes things too seriously.	_____
	Man	He is a vegetarian but he eats fish.	_____
3.	First speaker	She thinks the yoga instructor's diet is very healthy.	_____

Thinking about . . .

Health and fitness

How important is it to work to keep healthy? Do people think too much about their health? Read the sentences below. Write A if you agree, D if you disagree, and a question mark (?) if you are not sure.

1. _____ People should diet to improve their health, but not their appearance.

2. _____ It doesn't matter if we eat things we know are bad for us.

3. _____ Many people think about health too much and forget to have fun in their lives.

4. _____ Exercise is the key to good health.

5. _____ People should think about their mental health as much as they think about their physical health.

PRACTICE

Share your opinions with your partner.

> I don't think anything is more important than your health.

> I agree. But some people are way too careful about their health and forget to have fun. I think having fun helps keep you healthy!

www.nicetalkingwithyou.com

Share your opinions with people your age. Listen to Global Voices to hear what English speakers around the world have to say.

Personalities

Likes and dislikes

What would you like to change about your personality? Read the statements below. Check the meaning of any words you don't know. Write A if you agree and D if you disagree.

I want to be more . . .

rebellious. _____

confident. _____

honest. _____

friendly. _____

I want to be less . . .

impatient. _____

lazy. _____

stubborn. _____

timid. _____

 www.nicetalkingwithyou.com
Share your likes and dislikes with other people like you.

Words and phrases

Check the meaning of these words and phrases. Then use them to do the activities on the next page.

aggressive	generous	lazy	reserved
artistic	goofy	mature	serious
bookish	gossip	overachiever	skeptical
brave	honest	patient	smart
caring	humble	perfectionist	social butterfly
cheerful	impatient	polite	stubborn
confident	intelligent	powerful	timid
courageous	introvert	realistic	touchy
friendly	kind	rebellious	

Match it

Match the word on the left with the meaning on the right. Write the letter on the line. Check your answers with a partner.

1. _____ aggressive

2. _____ bookish

3. _____ introvert

4. _____ mature

5. _____ social butterfly

6. _____ touchy

a) adult-like in behavior or appearance

b) someone who is very sensitive about personal comments

c) someone who is very forceful

d) someone who reads a lot, especially serious books

e) a shy and quiet person

f) someone who is very comfortable making friends and often jumps from one group to another

Fill it in

Use the words and phrases on page 75 to complete the sentences. Then check your answers with a partner.

1. Emma is very _____; she's always drawing and creating beautiful things.

2. I wish she wasn't such an _____. It seems like she never takes it easy.

3. He is easy to be around, because he is so _____ and _____.

4. She loves to _____, so you can't tell her anything unless you want everyone to know.

5. As you get older, _____ things you did as a teenager start to seem _____.

6. Tim is a real _____ so he usually takes several tries to complete a task.

7. He has been tricked a lot, so he's pretty _____ of people nowadays.

8. Britney is not _____ at all, in fact she's quite outspoken.

Put it together

Draw a line to put the sentences together.

1. Lauren never gives herself enough credit because she's   really smart.

2. She's really confident about the test on Friday because she   so stubborn.

3. It's easy to teach Josh new things because he's   aced the practice.

4. My younger sister isn't very realistic, and she   really humble.

5. My colleague can be difficult to work with because he's   tends to dream big.

 Listen to check your answers.

Conversation questions

Who's a famous person you admire? Why?

What are your strong points?

Do you have any weaknesses?

Practice asking and answering the questions above with different partners.

Watch out!

Be careful not to make these common mistakes!

✘	✔
~~My strong point is friendly.~~	People say I'm friendly.
~~I wish I'm confident.~~	I wish I was more confident.
~~I think you're serious girl.~~	I think you're a serious person.

Practice saying these out loud so you can remember them!

Language point

Adjectives

I respect **honest** people.

People who are **confident** usually do well.

He's always **kind** to everybody.

Nouns

Some people think **honesty** can be a weakness.

She has the **confidence** to start a conversation with anybody.

I thanked her for her **kindness.**

PRACTICE

Read the sentences below. Write the correct form on the lines.

lazy/laziness	patient/patience	realistic/realist
rebellious/rebel	stubborn/stubbornness	

1. I admire people who have a lot of _____.

2. He doesn't like to do what other people say; he's quite a _____.

3. She's so _____. There's no way to change her mind.

4. My teacher told me there's no excuse for _____.

5. Let's just look at the facts and be _____.

Conversation strategies

Introducing a personal question

Use this phrase before asking someone a personal question.

Do you mind if I ask you something?

Do you mind if I ask you something?

No, not at all.

TIP Note that with *Do you mind . . .* questions, you should answer *No.* You can also answer with the expression *No, go ahead.*

Softening your response

Use this expression make your response sound softer and more indirect.

Well, I guess . . .

Do you mind if I ask you a question?

No, not at all.

How would you describe yourself?

Wow! Well, I guess I'm kind of talkative.

PRACTICE

Use the words and phrases on page 75 to describe three good characteristics about yourself and one bad one. Write them on the lines below. Then use these words and the expressions above to practice with a partner.

Good point   Bad point

1. _____   _____

2. _____

3. _____

Getting time to think

Use this phrase to give yourself time to think.

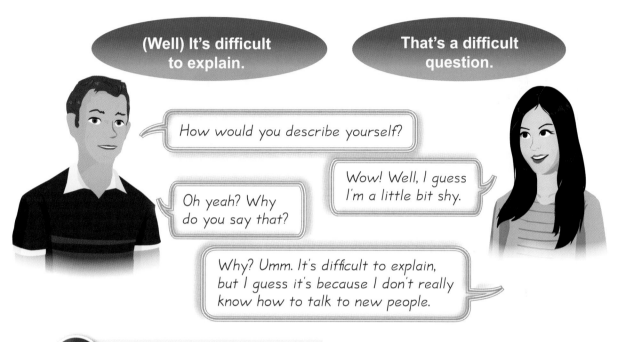

(Well) It's difficult to explain.

That's a difficult question.

How would you describe yourself?

Wow! Well, I guess I'm a little bit shy.

Oh yeah? Why do you say that?

Why? Umm. It's difficult to explain, but I guess it's because I don't really know how to talk to new people.

 TIP Use *Let me see, Let me think*, or *Hmm* if you need time to think.

PRACTICE

Write more information about your good and bad points in the spaces below. Then use the strategies on pages 78 and 79 and your ideas to practice with your partner, like in the example below.

Good / bad point	More information
shy	I don't know how to talk to people

A: Do you mind if I ask you something?

B: No, go ahead.

A: How would you describe yourself?

B: Umm. That's a difficult question.
   I guess I'm a bit lazy.

A: Really? Why do you say that?

B: Well, I usually leave my work till the last minute.
   And then I finish it as quickly as possible.

Conversation listening

A First listening

Do you recognize the famous people shown in the pictures below? Number the pictures in the order you hear about them. One is not used.

B Second listening

Which words do the speakers use to describe themselves? Circle A, B, or C.

1. **A** artistic   **B** energetic   **C** timid
2. **A** reserved   **B** brave   **C** intelligent
3. **A** self-made   **B** caring   **C** powerful
4. **A** average   **B** a perfectionist   **C** aggressive

C Noticing the conversation strategies

Listen for the expressions introduced on pages 78 and 79. Decide if the speakers think it's easy or difficult to explain themselves. Put checks (✔) in the boxes.

Conversation	Easy	Difficult
1.	☐	☐
2.	☐	☐
3.	☐	☐
4.	☐	☐

Get ready!

Organize your questions, answers, and vocabulary here to get ready for your *Personalities* conversation.

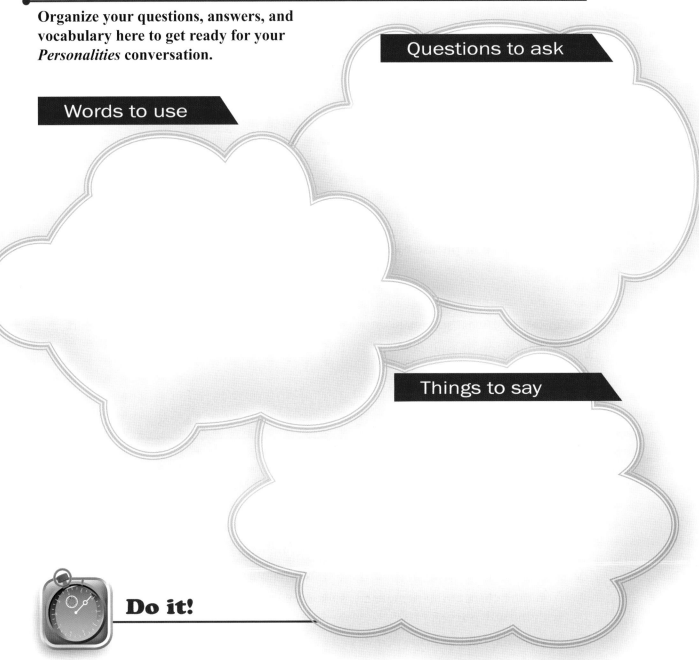

Questions to ask

Words to use

Things to say

Do it!

Practice some timed conversations with partners. When you hear something good, write it on this page after your conversation so you can remember it!

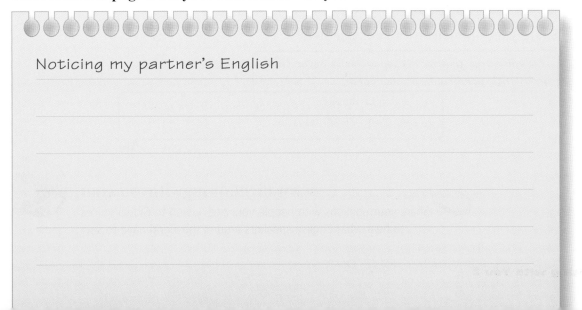

Noticing my partner's English

Real conversations

A Listening

Listen to five short conversations about people's personalities. Number the words or phrases below in the order you hear them.

a) _____ optimistic

b) _____ lazy

c) _____ approachable

d) _____ a hard worker

e) _____ impatient

f) _____ a leader

g) _____ trusting

h) _____ independent

B Vocabulary

Match the word or phrase with its meaning.

1. a sucker

2. at the last minute

3. measure of what success is

4. reach the top of your field

a) be very successful

b) someone who is easy to fool

c) the latest time possible to do something

d) a perfect example of success

Thinking about . . .

Looking at ourselves

Read the sentences below. Write 1–5. (1 means you strongly agree; 5 means you strongly disagree.)

1. You should never try to copy others. You must be yourself. _____

2. People with different personalities don't get on with each other. _____

3. If you want to be happy, you need to understand your character well. _____

4. You can't change your personality, so you must learn to be satisfied with the way you are. _____

5. Society and culture shape people's characters. _____

PRACTICE

Share your opinions with your partner.

> It seems to me that most people almost never think about their personality or character.

> I agree. But I believe it's a good idea to think about it to see what you can change.

www.nicetalkingwithyou.com

Share your opinions with people your age. Listen to Global Voices to hear what English speakers around the world have to say.

Careers

INTERNATIONAL CONFERENCE

Likes and dislikes

Do you have a full-time or part-time job? What do you like about it? Put checks (✔) in the boxes.

I like . . .

	😀	🙂	😐	🙁	😞
my job.					
my hours.					
my pay.					
my company.					
my co-workers.					
my boss.					
the building I work in.					
the area I work in.					

 www.nicetalkingwithyou.com
Share your likes and dislikes with other people like you.

Words and phrases

Check the meaning of these words and phrases. Then use them to do the activities on the next page.

accountant	classical musician	environmentalist	jeweler	police detective
actor	computer	fashion designer	journalist	professor
astronaut	programmer	flight attendant	lawyer	rock star
banker	construction	graphic artist	librarian	scientist
be successful	worker	help people	novelist	teacher
benefits	doctor	home office	nurse	telecommute
chef	editor	internship	pilot	therapist

Match it

Match the word on the left with the meaning on the right. Write the letter on the line. Check your answers with a partner.

1. _____ astronaut
2. _____ classical musician
3. _____ environmentalist
4. _____ journalist
5. _____ librarian
6. _____ therapist

a) someone who works to protect the natural world

b) someone who writes news stories for newspapers, magazines, TV, or radio

c) a person who works in a library

d) a person who is trained to help people with mental or physical problems

e) a person who plays traditional, serious music

f) a person who operates a spacecraft

Fill it in

Use the words and phrases on page 83 to complete the sentences. Then check your answers with a partner.

1. He got an unpaid _____ at a bank, and he's hoping to work there after he graduates.

2. Naoto is a successful _____ _____, and he designed the new packaging for my favorite bakery.

3. Rachael wants to become a college _____ because she likes to teach but doesn't have the patience for small children.

4. He isn't very realistic. He seems to think he can become a _____ _____ just by playing the guitar in his bedroom.

5. She's remodeling an empty bedroom into a _____ _____ so she can telecommute.

6. I want to be a nurse because I like to _____ _____.

7. My cousin wants to become a _____ _____, so she is always sketching and making her own clothes.

8. Kyle wanted to be a _____, but he has bad eyesight, so he became a flight attendant instead.

Put it together

Draw a line to put the sentences together.

1. James tried to be a construction worker,

2. Mai never studied geology,

3. He's interested in human rights,

4. She got a job in a publishing house,

5. Her boyfriend wants to be a doctor,

but she really wants to be a novelist.

but he's afraid the costs might be higher than the benefits.

but she became a diamond jeweler.

but he couldn't handle it.

so he's studying to be a lawyer.

Now listen to check your answers.

Conversation questions

> What would you like to do in the future?
>
> What are you good at?
>
> What's important to you about choosing a job?

Practice asking and answering the questions above with different partners.

Watch out!

Be careful not to make these common mistakes!

✗	✔
I don't get holiday	I don't get many holidays / days off.
I want good company.	I want to work at a good company.
I want enjoy.	I want to enjoy it / my job.

Practice saying these out loud so you can remember them!

Language point

will

If I get the chance, I **will** work abroad.

I hope I **will** get an interesting job with good co-workers.

would

If he could, he **would** work overseas for a few years.

If I became a reporter, I **would** write about human rights.

PRACTICE

Circle the correct word in italics.

1. I hope I *will* / *would* get a job where I can help people.

2. If I worked abroad, I *will* / *would* use my English skills.

3. If my sister was more realistic, she *won't* / *wouldn't* talk about becoming an astronaut.

4. I *will* / *would* become a banker or accountant if I was only interested in money.

5. If Steve passes the interview, he *will* / *would* start work next month.

Conversation strategies

Asking a favor

Use these phrases to ask someone for a favor.

Could I ask a favor?

Could you do me a favor?

Could I ask a favor?

Sure. What's up?

Describing the favor

Use these expressions to explain the favor you are asking.

I need your help with . . .

Could/Would you help me . . . ?

I wonder if it would be possible . . . ?

I need your help with a job application.

PRACTICE

Work with a partner. One is Student A, the other is Student B. Use the expressions above to ask your partner your favors.

Student A	Student B
Favor	**Favor**
Write a résumé	Write my essay
Check my English	Make a job application
Make a PowerPoint presentation	Write a letter of recommendation

Agreeing to help

Use these phrases to offer your help.

(Well,) I'll / OK. I'll try to / I'll do my best to / I'll see if I can help you.

I need your help with a job application.

Hmm. OK. I'll try to help you.

Great, thanks!

PRACTICE

Use your own ideas to write at least two more favors on the lines below.

Favor

Write a résumé

Check my English

Make a PowerPoint presentation

Write my essay

Make a job application

Write a letter of recommendation

Your ideas: _____

_____

_____

_____

Work with different partners. Use the expressions on pages 86 and 87 and the examples above to practice asking for favors and agreeing to help.

Conversation listening

A First listening

Listen to the conversations. What is the relationship between the speakers? Write 1–4 on the lines below. One is not used.

a) _____ parent and teacher

b) _____ parent and child

c) _____ teacher and student

d) _____ friends

e) _____ manager and worker

B Second listening

What favors are the people asking for? Number the pictures in the order you hear about them. One is not used.

C Noticing the conversation strategies

Listen to the expressions the speakers use to respond to the requests. When will they do the favors? Circle A or B.

1. **A** tonight   **B** tomorrow night

2. **A** next week   **B** Thursday

3. **A** by Monday   **B** by the end of the following week

4. **A** on Saturday   **B** on Sunday

Get ready!

Organize your questions, answers, and
vocabulary here to get ready for your
Careers conversation.

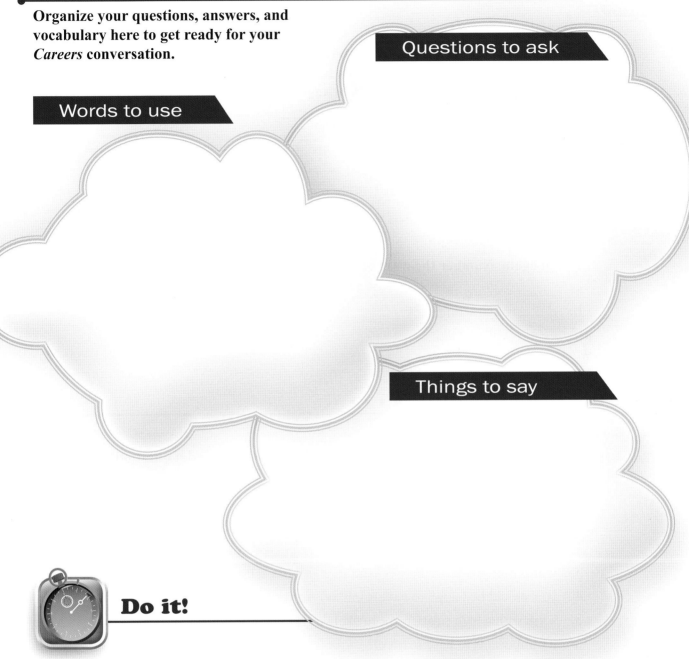

Questions to ask

Words to use

Things to say

Do it!

Practice some timed conversations with partners. When you hear something good,
write it on this page after your conversation so you can remember it!

Noticing my partner's English

Real conversations

A Listening

Listen to four short conversations about careers and skills. Would the speakers agree or disagree with the statements below? Write A if you think they would agree and D if you think they would disagree.

1. It's difficult to become a flight attendant. _____
2. Making dance routines and cooking are both fun, creative activities. _____
3. Becoming a movie director would be a dream come true. _____
4. Getting a good salary is much more important than job satisfaction. _____

B Vocabulary

Listen again. Number the words or phrases below in the order you hear them.

a) _____ cooking

b) _____ voice acting

c) _____ writing songs

d) _____ a business owner

e) _____ a flight attendant

f) _____ an interpreter

Thinking about . . .

Work and life

Read the questions below and write Y for Yes, N for No, and a question mark (?) if you aren't sure.

Do you think . . .

1. people should think more about their home lives than about their jobs? _____
2. it's natural for younger people to be paid less than older people? _____
3. you should work on the weekend if your boss asks you to? _____
4. you should be happy to have a job, no matter how bad it is? _____
5. a job with a high salary is more likely to bring you happiness? _____
6. it's important to have a career? _____

PRACTICE

Share your opinions with your partner.

> I believe that family is more important than work, but a career is more than just a job.

> So, you mean people should balance career and family equally?

www.nicetalkingwithyou.com

Share your opinions with people your age. Listen to Global Voices to hear what English speakers around the world have to say.

Personal entertainment

Likes and dislikes

What kind of entertainment do you enjoy at home? Look at the list of activities below. For each one, write A if you prefer doing it alone and F if you prefer doing it with friends.

watching TV _____

watching videos on the Internet _____

browsing the Internet _____

watching movies _____

playing computer games _____

reading books or magazines _____

www.nicetalkingwithyou.com
Share your likes and dislikes with other people like you.

Words and phrases

Check the meaning of these words and phrases. Then use them to do the activities on the next page.

card game	Facebook	nature documentary	role-playing game
cartoon	family show	paranormal	sitcom
commercial	fantasy game	programming	skill game
competition	fast-forward	puzzle	sports
cop show	game show	racing game	violence
DVR	high school drama	reality television	war game
e-book	medical drama	rerun	word game

Match it

Match the word on the left with the meaning on the right. Write the letter on the line. Check your answers with a partner.

1. _____ nature documentary
2. _____ competition
3. _____ reality television
4. _____ family show
5. _____ rerun
6. _____ sitcom

a) a program that people of all ages can watch

b) a comedy based on everyday life

c) a program shown on television again

d) a program that presents facts and information about plants, animals, or the earth

e) an event in which people try to win something

f) TV programs about actual life and real people, not actors

Fill it in

Use the words and phrases on page 91 to complete the sentences. Then check your answers with a partner.

1. Even though Sun is grown-up, she still loves to watch _____.

2. My father DVRs all his shows because that way he can _____ through the _____.

3. She hates the sight of blood, so she won't watch _____ _____.

4. Henry loves to play _____ _____ _____, so he's always sending me invites to join them.

5. My cell phone has puzzles and _____ _____ on it, and I like to play them on the train.

6. It's really easy to spend an hour on _____ just looking at friends' pictures and videos.

7. Lately there seem to be a lot more _____ shows – I guess people must really be into ghosts and mysteries.

8. My tablet has about 300 _____ on it, so I can take my library everywhere I go.

Put it together

Draw a line to put the sentences together.

1. Mom watches the news every night,

2. Max doesn't have a lot of free time,

3. Tammy says she only likes real card games

4. She doesn't often watch cop shows

5. Most evenings, he likes to stay home

because she doesn't like all the violence.

because the computer ones are too easy.

and play fantasy games on his computer.

but he spends it all playing war games.

and she never misses the weather forecast.

 Listen to check your answers.

Conversation questions

> What's your favorite TV program? Why?
> What do you watch online?
> What games do you like?

Practice asking and answering the questions above with different partners.

 Watch out!

Be careful not to make these common mistakes!

✘	✔
~~My best game is Super Mario.~~	My favorite game is Super Mario.
~~I like adventure game.~~	I like adventure games.
~~I don't like so much.~~	I don't like it/them (so) much.

Practice saying these out loud so you can remember them!

 Language point

during

During the video, my cell phone rang several times.

You need to concentrate ***during*** the game.

while

A lot of people surf the Internet on their smartphones ***while*** they watch TV.

I can watch a movie ***while*** I do my homework.

PRACTICE

Read the sentences below. Write *during* or *while* on the lines.

1. He fell asleep twice _____ the movie.

2. It's not a good idea to eat _____ you watch animal documentaries.

3. I always like to listen to music _____ I surf the Internet.

4. Juliana did all her homework _____ the commercials.

5. _____ I play this game I really need to focus, so can I ask you to keep the noise down?

Conversation strategies

Introducing a familiar topic

Use this phrase to introduce something you think your partner knows about.

> You know . . . , don't you?

> You know *The Simpsons*, don't you?

> Yes, of course. It's famous.

Asking for an opinion

Use this phrase to ask someone's opinion of something.

> What do you think of/about it?

> You know *The Simpsons*, don't you?

> Yes, of course. It's famous.

> What do you think of it?

Giving an opinion

Here are some more expressions you can use to give your opinion.

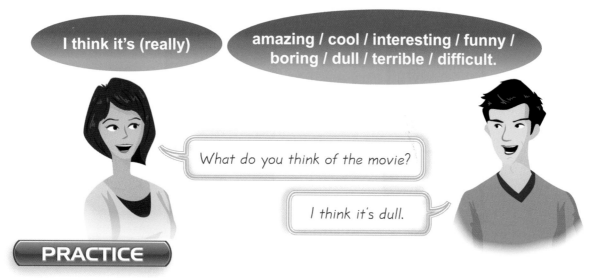

I think it's (really)

amazing / cool / interesting / funny / boring / dull / terrible / difficult.

What do you think of the movie?

I think it's dull.

PRACTICE

Fill in the blanks in the table below with the names of things you like and don't like. Then take turns and use your ideas to ask your partner's opinion, like in the examples on page 94.

Entertainment	Example	Like (✔)	Don't like (✘)
TV program			
Website			
Electronic game			
Online game			
Book or magazine			

Exploring the opinion

Use these expressions to find out more about your partner's opinions.

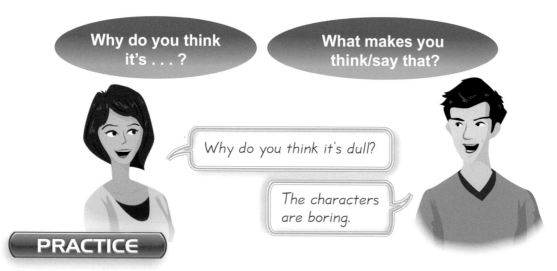

Why do you think it's . . . ?

What makes you think/say that?

Why do you think it's dull?

The characters are boring.

PRACTICE

Work with a new partner. Use the examples above to practice giving opinions and asking your partner for more information.

Conversation listening

A First listening

Listen to the conversations. What kind of entertainment are the speakers enjoying or talking about? Circle A or B.

1. **A**  **B**

2. **A**  **B**

3. **A**   **B**

4. **A**  **B**

B Second listening

Read the statements below. Decide if they are true or false. Write T if they are true and F if they are false.

1. _____ The man on the sofa watches the show often.
2. _____ The woman wants to try role-playing games next.
3. _____ They decide to play the game together.
4. _____ The man thinks it's bad that the woman doesn't use her tablet for school.

C Noticing the conversation strategies

How do the speakers describe their entertainment? What do they think of it? Put checks (✔) in the boxes.

Conversation	The speaker thinks it's . . .		
1.	☐ good	☐ horrible	☐ entertaining
2.	☐ moving	☐ stressful	☐ cool
3.	☐ boring	☐ difficult	☐ puzzling
4.	☐ amazing	☐ hopeless	☐ popular

Get ready!

Organize your questions, answers, and vocabulary here to get ready for your *Personal entertainment* conversation.

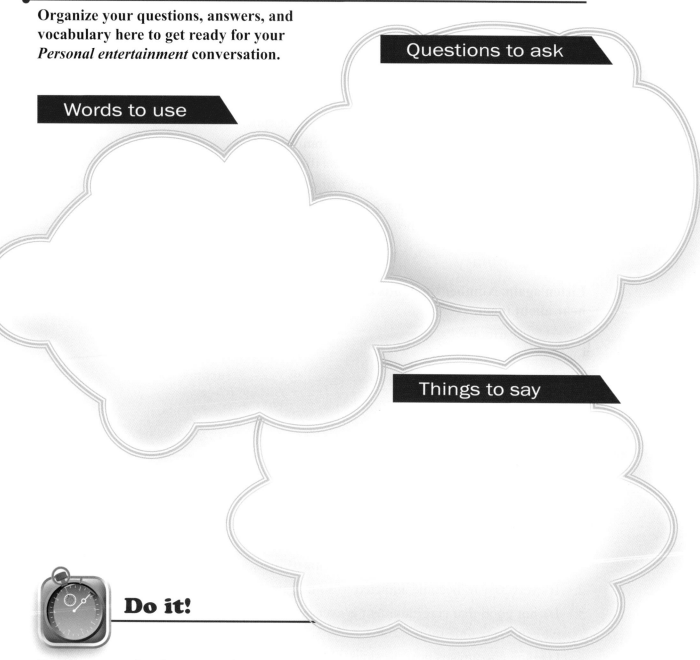

Words to use

Questions to ask

Things to say

Do it!

Practice some timed conversations with partners. When you hear something good your partners says, write on this page after your conversation so you can remember it!

Noticing my partner's English

Real conversations

A Listening

Listen to seven short conversations about entertainment. Decide if the statements below are true or false. Write T if they are true and F if they are false.

1. The speakers are talking about a regular mystery drama. _____
2. The man feels that watching TV is a waste of time. _____
3. Both women like to watch music programs on TV. _____
4. The men don't watch cartoons because they are childish. _____
5. Neither of the women likes to play games. _____
6. The woman thinks that playing online games is a good way to meet people. _____
7. The men enjoy playing the same computer game. _____

B Vocabulary

Listen again. Number the kinds of TV programs they talk about in the order you hear about them.

a) _____ cartoons
b) _____ comedies
c) _____ crime dramas
d) _____ news

e) _____ mystery dramas
f) _____ music programs
g) _____ sitcoms

Thinking about . . .

Entertainment

These days, the opportunities for entertainment are everywhere. Do you think that's a good thing? Read the sentences below and write 1–5. (1 means you strongly agree; 5 means you strongly disagree.)

1. Playing games and watching videos helps us relax. _____
2. It's very easy to become addicted to some games, and that is unhealthy. _____
3. It's not good that entertainment is everywhere these days because it means we can waste time more easily. _____
4. Gaming encourages positive skills, like problem-solving and using your imagination. _____
5. The violence in games doesn't make children more violent. _____
6. Governments want people to keep themselves entertained so they don't complain about problems in society. _____

PRACTICE

Share your opinions with your partner.

> It's great that there's so much entertainment available, but people don't know what to choose.

> I think there's too much available. It distracts us from more important things.

www.nicetalkingwithyou.com

Share your opinions with people your age. Listen to Global Voices to hear what English speakers around the world have to say.

Something special

Likes and dislikes

What things do you keep that connect you to important memories? Look at the list below. Circle Yes if you have this and No if you don't. You can add your own items to the list.

Things I keep . . .

letters	Yes	No
photos	Yes	No
an item of jewelry	Yes	No
a collection of something (what: _____)	Yes	No
an article of clothing	Yes	No
a charm	Yes	No
other: _____	Yes	No

www.nicetalkingwithyou.com
Share your likes and dislikes with other people like you.

Words and phrases

Check the meaning of these words and phrases. Then use them to do the activities on the next page.

antique	childhood	hand-me-down	one of a kind	souvenir
attached	collection	heirloom	pearls	special edition
autographed	diamond ring	keepsake	pocket watch	unique
copy	emotion	locket	postcard	vintage
bone china	family vacation	love letter	precious	
boxed set	fanboy	meaningful	rare	
brand-new	great-grandmother	medal	remind	

Match it

Match the word on the left with the meaning on the right. Write the letter on the line. Check your answers with a partner.

1. _____ great-grandmother
2. _____ locket
3. _____ medal
4. _____ rare
5. _____ autographed copy
6. _____ souvenir

a) very unusual
b) a creative work signed by the author
c) something you buy or keep to remember a place or event
d) a small piece of metal given as a reward for an achievement
e) the mother of a person's grandmother.
f) a small case usually with a picture in it, worn on a necklace or bracelet

Fill it in

Use the words and phrases on page 99 to complete the sentences. Then check your answers with a partner.

1. My mother has a special set of _____ _____ that she only uses on special occasions.

2. My fiancée wants a vintage wedding dress because she thinks _____ _____ things aren't meaningful.

3. The difference between a _____ and an heirloom is usually just a matter of value.

4. Brad bought his girlfriend an _____ ring because he thought it was more romantic.

5. She collects _____ from all the places she travels, so she always buys some to keep as well as some to mail.

6. Sean has a collection of _____ _____ of all his favorite movies.

7. Teresa really treasures the photos from her _____ _____. She says they remind her of growing up with her brothers.

8. I think she still has her _____ teddy bear, which looks pretty worn from years of attention.

Put it together

Draw a line to put the sentences together.

1. Dan loves the movie *Casablanca*
2. Her pearls came from her
3. Akio has always liked his uncle's
4. Anne has kept all of the love letters from her
5. He has collected lots of the

grandparents, so they are very precious to her.

so much he bought the special edition.

old boyfriends, but her husband doesn't like it.

goods because he is a total *Star Wars* fanboy.

pocket watches, and he wants to buy one.

🎧 Listen to check your answers.

Conversation questions

> What's one of your favorite things?
> Where did you get it?
> What makes it special to you?

Practice asking and answering the questions above with different partners.

Watch out!

Be careful not to make these common mistakes!

✗	✔
~~It's my special.~~	It's special to me.
~~I keep it forever.~~	I'll keep it forever.
~~It has deep mean.~~	It has a deep meaning.

Practice saying these out loud so you can remember them!

Language point

has/have + *verb*

Charlie ***has*** collected bottle caps for more than 10 years now.

Miki ***has*** always liked to make photo albums of her vacations.

used to + *verb*

I ***used to*** keep a journal when I was at high school.

This is the doll my mother ***used to*** play with when she was small.

PRACTICE

Read the sentences below. Write *has/have* or *used to* on the lines.

1. These earrings _____ been special to me for a long time.

2. My brother and I _____ buy old coins at the flea market.

3. That diamond ring _____ been in my family for 50 years.

4. I _____ collect CDs till I bought my MP3 player.

5. My mom _____ kept her wedding dress in this closet forever.

Conversation strategies

Starting an explanation

Use these expressions to check your partner is willing to listen to an explanation or story.

> **Hey,**
>
> **If it's OK, / all right,**
>
> **I want to**   **show you** / **tell you (about)**   **something.**

Hey, I want to show you something.

What is it?

Summarizing your comments

Use this expression to summarize your talk and show your partner that you will finish soon.

> **So, in other words . . .**

I want to tell you about my kimono. My parents bought it for me to wear for my coming-of-age ceremony. It's dark red with some floral design on it. Look.

Wow, it's beautiful!

I guess it was very expensive! So it's too bad I can't wear it much.

Yeah.

But in the future, if I have a daughter, I'll give it to her. So, in other words, it's my keepsake until I get married.

PRACTICE

Think of two items you can talk about and write about them on the lines below.

Object 1: _____

_____

Object 2: _____

_____

Making an inference

Use this to phrase to guess something about your partner or his or her topic from what he or she says.

It sounds like . . .

I listen to music every day. It makes me feel good.

It sounds like it's very important to you.

Yeah, I guess so.

PRACTICE

Read the sentences below and pick the response on the right that best matches it. Write the letter on the lines. Then check your answers with the class and take turns being A and B with a partner to practice.

A says:	B's response:
1. _____ I keep it locked in a drawer in my room.	a) It sounds like you can't live without it.
2. _____ I got it from my mother, who got it from her mother.	b) It sounds like you want to share it with the world.
3. _____ I usually wear it every day, even at night.	c) It sounds like you really want to keep it safe.
4. _____ I took a photo of it, which I use it as my profile picture.	d) It sounds like it's really important to your family.

Conversation listening

A First listening

Listen to the conversations. Number the pictures below in the order you hear about them. One is not used.

☐

☐

☐

☐

☐

B Second listening

Read the statements below and decide if they are true or false. Write T if they are true and F if they are false.

1. Her aunt used to wear a big ring to show she was strong. _____

2. She took a photo of a famous actress. _____

3. His grandfather thought that war had no meaning. _____

4. He and his brother used to watch baseball games together. _____

C Noticing the conversation strategies

Listen for the expression *It sounds like* and what the speakers infer. Write the missing words on the lines.

1. It made a big _____ on you.

2. She was a really _____ person.

3. Your grandfather was a _____ guy.

4. He was very _____ to you.

Get ready!

Organize your questions, answers, and vocabulary here to get ready for your *Something special* conversation.

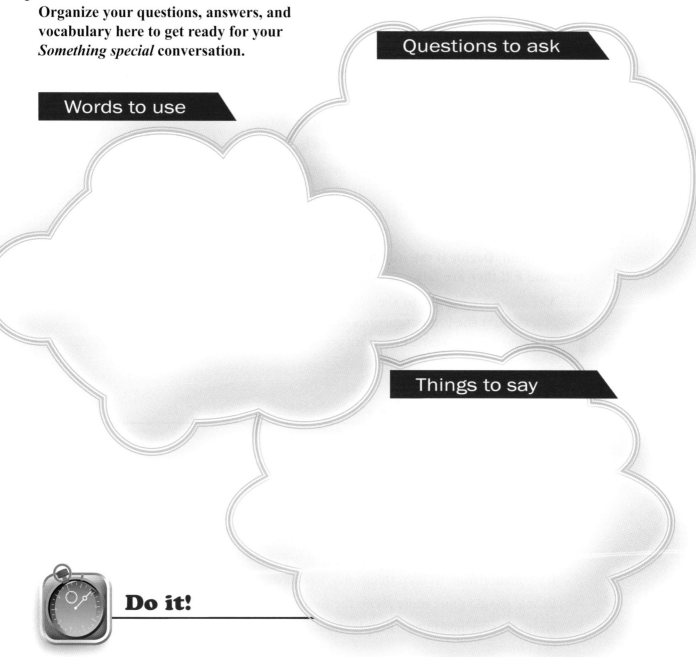

Questions to ask

Words to use

Things to say

Do it!

Practice some timed conversations with partners. When you hear something good, write it on this page after your conversation so you can remember it!

Noticing my partner's English

Real conversations

A Listening

Listen to three short conversations in which people talk about something special to them. Match the items on the left with the information about them on the right. One piece of information is not used.

1. _____ High-heel shoes
2. _____ Pearl earrings
3. _____ A ring

a) given by sister
b) given by his girlfriend
c) designed by an artist
d) given by parents

B Vocabulary

Listen again. Decide if the statements below are true or false. Write T if they are true and F if they are false.

1. The shoes are like art, so she only wears them on special occasions. _____
2. She thought she lost her earrings once and panicked. _____
3. The ring is a one-year anniversary present. _____

Thinking about . . .

Our keepsakes

Most people have some possessions that have special meaning to them. Read the opinions below and write A if you agree and D if you disagree.

1. Objects like charms and keepsakes have real power and should be treated with respect. _____

2. It's easy to become emotionally attached to something, and that's dangerous. _____

3. It's human nature to keep things that have special meaning to us. _____

4. People should think more about the future and less about the past. _____

5. Keepsakes are just things. People should care about other people, not objects. _____

6. Technology means people don't have real photos or letters anymore. That's bad. _____

 PRACTICE

Share your opinions with your partner.

> I don't think it makes any sense to keep old photos and letters and stuff.

> You're kidding, right? Keepsakes connect us with important feelings and people.

www.nicetalkingwithyou.com

Share your opinions with people your age. Listen to Global Voices to hear what English speakers around the world have to say.

Review 2

 # Conversation strategies

Unit 7

Can/Could I ask you something?/

I need some advice about . . . / I could really use your advice/help. / Can I get your advice on something?

Why don't you . . . / Maybe you should . . . / I think you should . . .

Unit 8

Speaking of . . .

Would you like it? / Can/Could you use it?

Thanks very much, but that's OK.

That's so nice of you, but I'll pass.

That's OK. But I appreciate the offer.

Unit 9

Do you mind if I ask you something ?

Well, I guess . . .

It's difficult to explain.

That's a difficult question.

Unit 10

Could I ask a favor? / Could you do me a favor?

I need your help with . . . / Could/Would you help me . . . ? / I wonder if it would be possible . . . ?

I'll help you. / OK, I'll try to / do my best to / see if I can help you.

Unit 11

You know . . . , don't you?

What do you think of/about it?

I think it's (really) amazing / cool / interesting / funny / boring / dull / terrible / difficult.

Why do you think it's . . . ? / What makes you think/say that?

Unit 12

Hey, / If it's OK, / all right, I want to show you something. / tell you about something.

So, in other words . . . / It sounds like . . .

A. **Review the conversation strategy expressions on page 107. Choose appropriate expressions for each of the four situations below and write them on the lines. Use your own ideas to make notes about each situation.**

Situation 1: Asking for advice

Person A: _____

Person B (response): _____

Notes: _____

Situation 2: Making an offer

Person A: _____

Person B (response): _____

Notes: _____

Situation 3: Asking a favor

Person A: _____

Person B (response): _____

Notes: _____

Situation 4: Asking for an opinion

Person A: _____

Person B (response): _____

Notes: _____

B. **Work with a partner. Take turns being A and B and practice having conversations for each situation. Try not to look at the book when you speak to your partner.**

LISTENING PRACTICE 1

A. Listen to the four conversations. Match the photos to the conversations. Write the number of the conversation in the box. One photo is not used.

☐ ☐ ☐

☐ ☐

B. Listen again. In each conversation the speaker asks a question or makes an offer. How does the other speaker respond? Put checks (✔) in the boxes.

Conversation	Speaker's response	
1.	☐ gives advice	☐ doesn't give advice
2.	☐ agrees to do favor	☐ doesn't agree to do favor
3.	☐ accepts offer	☐ doesn't accept offer
4.	☐ gives advice	☐ doesn't give advice

SPEAKING PRACTICE 2

Review the topics you covered in Units 7 to 12. Choose three from the list below and check (✔) the boxes.

Unit	Topic
☐ Experience abroad	living and working or studying abroad; advice
☐ Health	health and fitness; offers
☐ Personalities	different kinds of people; personal questions
☐ Careers	jobs and careers; favors
☐ Personal entertainment	home entertainment; opinions
☐ Something special	important possessions; explanations

Practice having conversations about your topics with different partners. Use the expressions below to link your ideas and sentences.

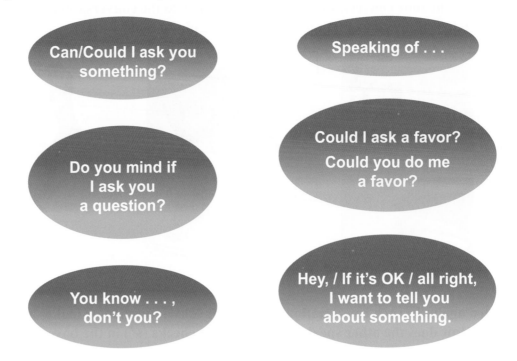

Can/Could I ask you something?

Speaking of . . .

Do you mind if I ask you a question?

Could I ask a favor?
Could you do me a favor?

You know . . . , don't you?

Hey, / If it's OK / all right, I want to tell you about something.

LISTENING PRACTICE 2

A. Listen to the three conversations. Decide which statement below best summarizes each conversation. Circle A or B.

1. **A** The man liked the experience, but the woman didn't.

    B The man didn't like the experience, but the woman did.

2. **A** Sarah believes in herself and works hard.

    B Sarah thinks her friend should try to be more confident.

3. **A** The guitar pick is a reminder of the band's first concert.

    B The guitar pick is a reminder of how lucky he is.

B. Listen again. The speakers use the expressions below. Match the expressions to the conversations. Write the letter on the line. One is not used.

Conversation

1. _____

2. _____

3. _____

Expression

a) *Do you mind if I ask you a question?*

b) *Could you do me a favor?*

c) *You know . . . , don't you?*

d) *I want to show you something.*

Appendix
Conversation strategies

Unit 1

Excuse me . . .

Wow, long time no see! / It's been a while. /
a long time. / ages.

How are things? / How have you been?

Anyway, I guess I should go. / Well, I better
get going.

Nice talking with you. / Great seeing you again.

Unit 2

Well you know . . .

You should come over sometime. / when you're
free. / when you're not too busy.

I'd love to/that. / That would be great. / Good
idea! / Sounds great.

Unit 3

Oh, before I forget . . .

Let me give you this. / I want to give you
something. / This is for you. / This is from me
and my friends.

You shouldn't have! / Thanks so much. /
I (really) appreciate it.

Unit 4

I have an idea!

If you have time, let's . . . / If you're not so busy,
let's . . . / If you're free, how about . . .

Sounds good. / Sure, I'd love to.
When/Where do you want to meet/go?

Well, that's a great idea, but . . . / Um, I'd love to,
but . . . / Well, thanks, but . . .

Unit 5

By the way . . .

Nice / cool / cute . . .

What do you mean?

I mean . . . / What I mean is . . .

Unit 6

You know what?

Could/Can I borrow this? / Do you think I could
borrow this? / Would it be OK if I borrowed this?

I'll give it back next week. / I won't lose it,
I promise. / I'll take good care of it.

Sure, go ahead. / Be my guest. / Yeah,
no problem.

Unit 7

Can/Could I ask you something?

I need some advice about . . . / I could really
use your advice/help. / Can I get your advice
on something?

Why don't you . . . / Maybe you should . . . /
I think you should . . .

Unit 8

Speaking of . . .

Would you like it? / Can/Could you use it?

Thanks very much, but that's OK.

That's so nice of you, but I'll pass.

That's OK. But I appreciate the offer.

Unit 9

Do you mind if I ask you something?

Well, I guess . . .

It's difficult to explain.

That's a difficult question.

Unit 10

Could I ask a favor? / Could you do me
a favor?

I need your help with . . . / Could/Would you
help me . . .? / I wonder if it would be
possible . . . ?

I'll help you. / OK, I'll try to / do my best to /
see if I can help you.

Unit 11

You know . . . , don't you?

What do you think of/about it?

I think it's (really) amazing / cool /interesting /
funny / boring / dull / terrible / difficult.

Why do you think it's . . . ? / What makes you
think/say that?

Unit 12

Hey, / If it's OK / all right, I want to show you
something. / tell you about something.

So, in other words . . . / It sounds like . . .